POULSEN ON THE ROSE

POULSEN ON THE ROSE

SVEND POULSEN

Translated by
C. Campbell McCallum

THE GARDEN BOOK CLUB
121 CHARING CROSS ROAD
LONDON, W.C.2

FIRST PUBLISHED DENMARK 1941
REVISED 1954
FIRST PUBLISHED ENGLAND 1955

This edition is published by arrangement with
MACGIBBON & KEE LTD.

Printed in Great Britain
by Robert Cunningham and Sons Ltd.
Alva, Scotland

Contents

Illustrations

Preface

A NUMBER OF YEARS have come and gone since the publication in this country [Denmark] of a book on the subject of roses. And as roses, like every other living thing, are ever subject to change and development, the need for an up-to-date work on roses would seem to be called for.

The great developments that have taken place in this special field during the past twenty-five years are undoubtedly worthy of record. In some cases many new kinds of roses have been imported, and in others, entirely new types have been evolved. Moreover, as from my earliest youth I have enjoyed exceptional opportunities for following these developments stage by stage, I cannot but feel that the time has now arrived for me to share the knowledge thus gained with others.

In a country like Denmark where most people live in close contact with Mother Earth, either personally or through the medium of friends and relatives, to be the owner of, or to be able to lease a bit of land, seldom presents any great difficulty. And as one could hardly imagine a garden (albeit laid out essentially for growing food) without room for a few rose bushes, or at least a tiny rose-bed, it may be said without exaggeration that the growing of roses has become everyman's hobby. The cultivation of plants, and especially of roses, is as healthy an occupation for soul and body as

7

any other form of activity, though if this were the only advantage to be gained from it the writing of the present book would hardly be necessary.

But rose-growing is definitely much more than merely a healthy pastime. It may, indeed, become the most interesting and pleasurable of occupations, sharpening one's powers of observation and improving one's sense of colour and beauty. Moreover, it not only brings beauty and pleasure to the grower himself, but to everyone entering his garden-gate, and every chance passer-by.

A rose-grower, collector or rose enthusiast is not like other collectors who shut themselves up and lock away their treasures. On the contrary, he possesses such an abundance of prizes that he can afford to distribute much of his wealth; for his skill and knowledge carry their own reward within themselves. The greater the effort and enthusiasm of the grower the more productive and profitable will their roses become in return.

Roses can be grown almost anywhere. There ought to be roses, and indeed there *are* roses everywhere in the gardens of Denmark. In days of old June was the pre-eminent month for roses. That was in the long bygone days of Frederik VI before roses had been taught to bloom all summer through. June is still *the* rose month, of course, for then it is that they all burst into flower, the old as well as the newer types; all the wild and all the ramblers. The air is filled with their enchanting fragrance, and during this one month we all live in an ecstasy of roses. For, even should one happen to have no garden of one's own it is never far to a nearby villa-road. There you find them flowering not only in the front garden but bursting out into the road over fence or wall, blazing with colour, for everyone to see and enjoy. This is our Town, and this is our Land, with its towns, villages and roadways. And thus may they flower always, freely, gorgeously, under a blazing June sun!

So I wrote in 1941, and now I have nothing more to add beyond the fact that during the years that have elapsed since then so many new arrivals have appeared in the world of roses that a new edition of my book on roses seems doubly imperative.

Fortunately the main centres for rose-growing and for the raising of new types in England, France, Germany, America and many other countries are now once more open to us. And so many new types have been created that a revision of existing lists is long overdue; some items must be added, others deleted. The illustrations, too, must be renewed to include some of the more prominent of the new-comers.

Certain passages have had to be entirely re-written, for much is now known about cultivation which it is my wish to share with my readers.

S. P.

CHAPTER ONE

Wild Roses
and the First Cultivated Varieties

THE ORIGINAL HOME OF ALL WILD ROSES was in the Northern Hemisphere. Their territory stretched from Northern Scandinavia to Southern Europe and North Africa, from Kamschatka and Siberia to India and Persia, and from Canada to Florida. Roses were originally never found growing wild south of the Equator, but later found their way, by colonisation, to even the most distant areas, and are now distributed practically everywhere on the globe where the white man has established himself.

Whenever a plant genus is spread over so large an area with such widely differing conditions of growth, and is subject to such differences of climate it cannot but be influenced thereby.

The genus *Rosa* is therefore immensely rich in types, many of which have gradually found way into our gardens, where they seem to flourish equally well whether collected on American prairies, among the highlands of Tibet or China, in Japan with its friendly island climate, in semi-Arctic regions, or from India, Persia, the Caucasus or Southern Europe. It is, however, more especially the hardy kinds from the Far North, from Central Asia and the temperate zone which are of most importance to us, the kinds originating from more southern climes being less hardy, having their chief justification as under-stocks for our large-flowered and perpetual garden roses.

The single-flowered briar rose is of singular beauty. In spite of its short flowering season beginning, with some kinds, towards the end of May, and with others at the close of June or even July, they provide us, with their varied growth, flowers, leaves, thorns and hips with an ever-varying and suitable plant material which may be put to good use in our parks and gardens. But, whether used as standards, hedgerows or free-growing bushes on our lawns, or as a natural background to, or frame around the rose-garden, or, as is the case with our own wild dog-rose, a vigorous under-stock for cultivated roses, it must naturally find place in a book dealing with roses, for it is the main progenitor of all the multifarious types in the world of beauty with which we shall attempt to make our readers familiar.

ROSA CANINA (dog-rose) is our own wild briar, the one we see growing everywhere along rustic roadsides or skirting woodland coppices, where, clinging to trees and other bushes, or climbing over and among them and hooking themselves fast with their sturdy thorns, they take on the appearance of a rambler. In this way it may reach quite a respectable height and adorn its host tree or bush with a wealth of midsummer bloom. As a free-growing pillar it forms a large but graceful overhanging bush.

Rosa canina grows wild over large areas of Europe and Scandinavia, and is completely hardy. It is used almost exclusively as a seed plant from which to grow under-stocks for cultivated garden roses. (See chapter on Propagation of Roses.)

The flowers and the colour of the leaves of *Rosa canina* vary considerably, and as the seed of each remains true to type it is possible to select individual plants with special characteristics, such as shiny healthy foliage or strong growth, etc., with which to work up large scale culture of types that are more suitable for use as understocks than the coarse mixture that would result from collecting seed at random. Mr Aksel Olsen, the owner of a nursery at Kolding [Denmark] has cultivated and given to the trade two specially fine specimens which he calls *Rosa canina mosvig* and *Rosa canina skamling*. Both are of a strong clean pink colour. He describes how when he used to go rambling across the Downs at Skamlingsbanken he found an area a few kilometres from the summit of the highest hill containing exceptionally fine variations of *Rosa canina*, which seem to foregather specially in that district, and how, from among them, he selected the two choicest specimens.

An English variety, *Rosa canina andersonii*, possesses the largest and brightest pink colour of all dog-roses. It has a charming smell and forms a thorny bush some four to six feet in height, covered in winter with brilliant scarlet hips.

ROSA WARDII CULTA resembles most of all a plain Canina in growth. It was brought to Europe from South Eastern Tibet by Mr Kingdon Ward in 1924. It forms an attractive elegant bush about six feet high. The olive-green stems and light delicate foliage, the pure white single flowers, and the red stigma surrounded by cream-coloured stamens give this little-known plant its distinctive stamp.

A Swedish botanist puts forward the theory that *Rosa canina* is not a species but a form-class of many varying kinds.

It is strange that *Rosa canina* has had little or no influence on the formation and appearance of cultivated roses. *Rosa canina x Jacqueminot* is one of the few hybrids that is on the market in this country [Denmark]. It may be as much as nine feet high, has healthy glossy leaves, large dark carmine single flowers, and is later covered with showers of large decorative dark red-lacquer hips. On account of its hardiness and strong growth it is also used as a stock and stem for high standard roses.

ROSA RUBIGINOSA (sweet-briar). In Denmark this is known as 'apple-rose'—a name that in England is given to *Rosa pomifera*. The reason for the Danish name is that, towards evening or before rain, the leaves and young sprouts of *Rosa rubiginosa* diffuse the pleasant, bitter-sweet smell of apple. It grows wild over most of Europe and is found also in Persia. It has always found favour in our gardens especially as a hedge, for which it is singularly well suited —above all on a light soil. It is a thoroughly healthy and hardy rose, and one that may reach a ripe old age. Thus, it is related that, when an old rose bush of this species was cut down its annual rings proved it to be 120 years old, although the plant showed not the smallest sign of disease and had always been known for its hardiness and vigour. Sweet Briar or Eglantine is a delightful, graceful bush with a profusion of medium large bright pink blooms followed by equally as many fat oval hips, which ripen in October. Its foliage has five or seven leaflets, light and dainty and, as mentioned before, sweetly fragrant. It is of erect growth and very prickly. There are a number of extremely beautiful garden varieties of the Sweet Briar that are suitable either for the rose-bed or grown as solitary bushes. It is Lord Penzance's hybrids that more than any other have retained the character, growth and perfume of the wild rose, and they may be recommended together with some later comers as some of our best garden shrubs. There are varieties like the dark carmine-red Anne of Gierstein, the light pink Bradwardine, the two yellow-red types Lord and Lady Penzance, and the low tightly branched variety, *Magnifica*. The Sweet Briar forms an excellent under-stock for many of the wild and older type garden roses.

ROSA RUBRIFOLIA is a native of the Pyrenees and other southern European mountains. It reminds us in many respects of *Rosa canina*, but is, however, distinguished by its reddish foliage, its small red flowers gathered in umbels and by its somewhat smaller fruit.

Were it not that this rose, which is somewhat susceptible to rose rust when grown on clay soils, is such an excellent hedging plant, and that even on exposed sites, it would never have been considered worthy of inclusion among the select company of the most suitable and best wild roses for Danish conditions.

ROSA CAROLINA is one of America's good wild roses that has found place in our gardens. It grows wild all over eastern America, from Canada to Florida, and is quite common on moist soils. With its erect, vigorous growth, often reaching as much as nine feet in height, with its red-brown stems and its persistent red hips that remain attached to the plant all winter through, it is also, outside its blooming season—which falls quite late—a useful plant for our parks and gardens. The blooms are pink set in half umbels.

ROSA VIRGINIANA (*Rosa humilis lucido*). This hardy American wild rose is to be found all along the American coast from Newfoundland to Pennsylvania and was the first American rose to be brought to Europe. It forms an erect shrub from three to six feet high. The stems are red-brown when sprouting. The blooms are bright pink growing singly, or more rarely in clusters. Its foliage is dainty and closely packed, and it is an excellent hedge and bedding plant even under quite mediocre conditions. Its hips are of medium size, being round and numerous, and this latter feature, in conjunction with the attractive harvest colour of the foliage, give the plant a heightened colour effect among surrounding garden neighbours. There is also a white variety, *R. virginiana alba*.

ROSA SPINOSISSIMA (*Rosa pimpinellifolia;* Scotch or Burnet rose). This species is found spread over most of Scandinavia, Ireland, England, most of Europe, Siberia and Central Asia, but is not found in the Himalayan district.

On account of the great diversity of locations with their accompaning differences of climate, the guise and growth of this plant also differ considerably. In this country [Denmark] it is a low, tightly-branched, small-leaved prickly bush which spreads itself abroad by means of runners, that is especially suitable for planting on sandy soils.

In gardens it is much used for low hedges. Our native spinosissima has single, yellow-white or faintly pink blooms. The fruit is round and dark-brown, with reflexing calyx; it is the smallest of the wild rose species we know. There are, however, also taller forms such as *Rosa spinosissima altaica*. Since olden times the type has been widely grown, especially in Scotland, where it is said to have become almost a national flower. Moreover, there are numbers of garden hybrids of venerable or later date, and many of them are of astonishing daintiness and beauty both in form, colour and fragrance. Stanwell's Perpetual is specially well suited for planting as a perpetual flowering hedge. It is slightly double, and pale rose in colour. Among other good sorts with double blooms there is the pink shaded Lady Hamilton; *lutea pleno* with yellow and *purpurea* with reddish-purple flowers.

Among later varieties of *Rosa spinosissima* hybrids there

is reason to mention Kordes' Frühlingsgold—semi-double, golden yellow; Frühlingsmorgen, also semi-double but carmine red. These are extremely vigorous and lavishly flowering garden shrubs.

ROSA FOETIDA (*Rosa lutea;* Austrian briar or Austrian yellow) arrived in Europe towards the close of the sixteenth century. It is widely diffused throughout China, Asia Minor, Persia and Turkestan and is also found in Afghanistan. Indeed, it has been known and grown in Denmark for several centuries. Of colour it is the purest yellow or golden-yellow rose we know; its blooms are single, its leaves small and of a brownish-green shade, and it is armed with numbers of sharp thorns. Although this rose is completely hardy, it requires a warm site if it is to develop its full strength and beauty. If conditions are right, however, it yields more with its firework display of dazzling yellow during its short blooming period early in June than many perpetuals ever develop through a whole summer. *Rosa foetida's* near relation *Rosa foetida bicolor* (Austrian Copper, or the Capucine Rose), a single yellow with a copper-red back, has been known and cultivated since 1596. Also Persian Yellow and Harrison's Yellow with their double yellow or ochre-yellow blooms are of the same origin. The celebrated rose-gardener Pernet-Ducher was successful, about 1900, in crossing the strong colour of these roses into the Hybrid Teas, which have since been called Pernetianas, in honour of their originator. The first of these sorts, Soleil d'Or, Rayon d'Or and Juliet, were pure Pernetianas with all their faults, proving regrettably frail and very susceptible to black spot.

It may be said that the original pernetiana strain no longer exists, as, by persistently crossing the brilliant orange and yellows of the pernetianas with Hybrid Teas, a new type of the latter, of which Peace, Spek's Yellow and President Herbert Hoover are good examples, has evolved.

B

ROSA HUGONIS is one of the really good garden plants that seems to feel comfortable under all conditions. It has light dainty foliage and carries masses of light yellow single blooms. It bears small black hips and keeps its foliage, which often retains its attractive harvest shade, until far into autumn.

I have planted it in my garden among white-thorn and sweet briar where, in spite of its extraordinary wealth of bloom, its cascades of pale-yellow single blooms and bright airy foliage give the entire shrub an exceptionally light and graceful effect. It is completely hardy, surviving even the arctic winter temperatures of 1940.

CANTABRIGIENSIS (*Rosa Hugonis x sericea*). Though not as canary-yellow as *Hugonis*, it surpasses it in growth and size of blooms. It forms graceful bushes, often as much as eight feet high, flowers in May, and carries orange-coloured hips.

ROSA HELENAE from central China is an exceptionally beautiful, vigorous bush with shiny attractive foliage and clustering white flowers. Its hybrid—*Helenae hybrida*—is even more beautiful and is, moreover, more hardy than the actual species. In June it is a typical overhanging bush covered with charming yellow-white or pure white small flowers, and carrying, until far into the winter, equally many small tile-red hips. This description might also apply to *Rosa multiflora* were it not for a difference of growth. *Helenae* is more vigorous, more erectly pendant and retains its foliage longer into autumn. In *Helenae* the flowers carry an air of grace and pure white chastity to be found in no other wild rose. Moreover, it smells delightfully. It suffered but little damage from the frosts of 1940.

ROSA MULTIFLORA. Also known and described under the designation *Rosa polyantha*—is a native of Japan. It was introduced to England in 1875, but had been previously grown in France.

Rosa multiflora is an erect vigorous bush with light green foliage and bark. The blooms form compact clusters, often as much as 12 inches long. They are small and single and are followed in autumn by cheery, small, coral-red hips. *Rosa multiflora* is the parent of many of our cultivated roses such as the hardy ramblers Aglaia, Tausendschön and Crimson Rambler. The latter which was found in Japan, is assumed to be a result of cross-pollination with *Rosa chinensis*, and counts among its progeny also the Poulsen roses.

Rosa multiflora is hardy in Denmark. In addition to being used as an under-stock for polyantha and rambler varieties, it is a charming park rose whether employed either as a hedge, a solitary bush, or to cover a suitable slope where it looks charming with its wealth of flowers and its showers of crimson hips.

ROSA MOSCHATA (musk rose), found growing wild from Afghanistan to Cashmere, has been known and grown in Southern Europe from quite ancient times. Sir George Watt describes it as he saw it in the Himalayas as follows: 'It is far and away the most beautiful and most vigorous of all Himalayan roses, it mounts over wayside bushes and over small woodland trees fringing the forests and there forms a dense dome-like bush which, when in bloom, reminds one of hummocks of snow. Its brilliant flowers are the joy of bee and bird and it fills the air with a fragrance which cannot be imagined by anyone who has not lived, during early summer, in the invigorating air of these mountains.'

In this country, too, this rose is of considerable value, but it requires plenty of room and preferably a warm, light soil and a sheltered site.

It has quite large single white flowers, clustered together in flat open umbels. It is extraordinarily vigorous, but, despite all these advantages, would not have been included in this book were it not for the fact that it is the mother of the charming Noisette ramblers, so well known in our gardens, such as: Rêve d'Or, Céline Forestier, and William Allen Richardson.

Latterly a series of richly-flowering and more perpetual flowering hybrids of *Rosa moschata* have been evolved by crossing it with various large-flowered garden roses. These may almost be accepted as perpetual flowering park roses. They have come much into use in England, but are not quite hardy in this country [Denmark]. Hamburg is one of these. See chapter on Ramblers.

It suffered considerably during last winter's frosts but fortunately retained a few shoots unharmed and flowered well from these in June 1940.

ROSA WICHURAIANA was found between 1859 and 1861 by the German botanist Wichura in China and Japan and came to Europe via America.

On arrival here *Rosa Wichuraiana* aroused considerable attention on account of its singularly vigorous creeping growth which makes it so specially suitable for covering large slopes. Its shiny green foliage—which in many ways reminds one of box—and its late flowering season—far into July—quickly gave rise to its being used as a parent for an entirely new type of ramblers which now, with Dorothy Perkins at their head, almost dominate our gardens.

Even so widely planted a rose as Ellen Poulsen has on the paternal side (Dorothy Perkins), *Rosa Wichuraiana's* blood in its veins. Its flowers are small, pure white and numerous, growing mainly in clusters. They diffuse an enchanting fragrance—one of the special characteristics of this species, and one which will be recognised also in Ellen Poulsen. It stood the winter well when crawling over the ground and covered with snow, but when bound upright it froze back badly—without however being killed outright—as were most of its daughters.

ROSA SETIGERA (American prairie rose) is the most hardy and at the same time the most vigorous of all ramblers. In its wild growing form it can only be employed in exceptionally roomy conditions. Its foliage is greenish grey with pale-pink single flowers. Formerly this species was of importance as the parent of several good hardy ramblers, e.g. Queen of the Prairies, Baltimore Belle and several others, which before our *multiflora* and *Wichuraiana* hybrids appeared, were much in favour. American cultivators have now taken it up again in renewed cross-pollination experiments and, as an initial result, have given us such varieties as the widely planted and almost completely hardy (also in this country, even during the arctic winter of 1940) Dr W. van Fleet and American Pillar.

It is now almost impossible to determine the pedigree of our various ramblers. They are so crossed and intercrossed that their original individual characteristics have become ever less distinct. But, however that may be, there is little doubt that our rose population is being steadily and greatly improved.

ROSA SETIPODA. On its native soil, Hupeh in China, this species appears as a lofty almost rambling bush with annual shoots of up to four yards in length. In my garden near Copenhagen it seldom reached more than six feet high, but it certainly formed an attractive bush with its wealth of clustering blooms, often combining as many as twenty-five individual flowers in each cluster; the colour is pink with a lighter centre and sharply drawn pistils. The foliage is light and healthy. The shoots are armed with powerful, sharp thorns. It has proved hardy in this country—even in 1940.

ROSA OXYODON (*amblyotis*) is strangely enough, a seldom-mentioned and little-grown wild rose. Personally I would warmly recommend it. With its moderate growth, its greyish leaves, its numberless large bright crimson flowers and its round, durable, shining red hips, it is undoubtedly an excellent garden, hedge, or bush rose that can safely be planted in an exposed spot in the beach garden, or in the fringe of your shelter belt; thanks to its runners it quickly forms a dense stand.

ROSA OMEIENSIS is found in Sikkim, Burma and China, where it grows at heights varying from nine to twelve thousand feet. The young shoots are round, smooth, and red, and under each leaf-bud they sprout a couple of big curved shiny reddish-brown thorns ending in a serviceable barb. On the older branches the thorns are round, straight and uncomfortably sharp.

One of this plant's most distinctive characteristics is that the flowers have very short stalks and are carried on small thin lateral shoots on the main stem. They are small, pure white, and sometimes faintly pink towards the centre. Its hips—about the size of a pea—are red and smooth.

ROSA OMEIENSIS PTERACANTHA is the form most often planted in this country. It differs from the usual wild rose in having still bigger, broader, curiously bewinged thorns which, on the young shoots, are bright red and transparent. Even without its flowers this plant is of great beauty and especially so when the sun's rays are caught by its pellucid coral-red thorns.

It blooms early in May and is, together with the next mentioned *Rosa Willmottiae*, generally among the first in the field.

Last winter in many places it froze down to the ground but sprouted vigorously anew next spring with its young (and even without flowers) very beautiful shoots.

ROSA WILLMOTTIAE is a widely distributed, many stemmed bush which may reach from three to six feet or more in height. The thorns are light brown; the nine leaflets are small, smooth and toothed. With its long overhanging shoots, densely covered with light, purplish-pink small flowers, it presents a cheery bright picture towards the end of May. Like so many other valuable plants it was collected by Wilson in South West China near the Tibetan border. It is quite hardy.

ROSA RUGOSA is common in Japan, eastern Siberia, Kamchatka and northern China, where it is found growing in sandy soils along coastal districts. It is easily the most self-sufficient and most hardy of all wild roses. Well suited, as it is, for planting on even the most meagre of soils, it has found place in many of our seaside gardens right out on the sea shore where, by means of its runners, it quickly spreads through the sandy soil and forms dense stools which, thanks to the robust dark-green foliage, seem to stand up to the wind better than do most other plants.

Its branches are thickly covered with tiny prickles; the flowers, which are gathered in small sprays, are quite large, single, and red, or occasionally white. It commences to bloom quite early in June and continues with repeating flowers throughout the rest of the summer, the numerous large meaty hips being thus often seen simultaneously with newly opening flowers.

From *Rosa rugosa*, in the course of time, numbers of good hardy garden roses have been evolved. First those that resemble the wild form most nearly and which are thus also the most hardy. Frau Dagmar Hastrup, pink, single; Stella Polaris, white, single; both carrying a rich harvest of large meaty hips. Then we have Blanc Double de Coubert, white, double; Souvenir de Christophe Cochet, with large double, dark-red blooms; also bouquet and small-flowered kinds like Signe Relander, dark red; F. J. Grootendorst, carmine, and Pink Grootendorst, of a pale rosy shade.

Like the mother species they all form large spreading

three to six feet high shrubs, while the next category of *rugosa* roses, those which most nearly approach the large-flowered garden roses, may easily reach the same height as the mother kind, but may also be frozen back in winter and, in any case, they are always at their best when cut back and thinned out each succeeding year.

Then there is the oldest *rugosa* of all; the light pink Conrad Ferdinand Meyer; the yellowish-red Dr Eckener and the yellow Goldener Traum.

The former importance of *Rosa rugosa hollandica* as a stock for our garden roses has now much declined and will undoubtedly soon die out altogether. In this country it is no longer used for this purpose. It is much used in England as a stock for standard rose trees.

ROSA MOYESII was first generally known and grown after E. H. Wilson, who collected plants for the well-known London nurseries, James H. Veitch and Son, found it in China and brought back the seed to England. It is named after the China missionary, J. Moyes, who was of considerable assistance to Wilson while he was searching for rare plants in the district between Mount Omi and Tatien-lu near the Tibetan border. *Rosa Moyesii* was found at heights varying between 6,000 and 8,000 metres.

In 1933 I described this plant in my note-book in the following way: 'Rosa Moyesii and its near relation, Fargesii, are hardy, have the same eleven-leafletted dainty pale leaves and the same vigorous growth. The former variety is as deep red as ox-blood, the latter varying from carmine to rose red. Both have pretty, durable, coral-red, bottle-shaped hips.' I wrote further: 'I have planted a wilderness of roses behind my dwelling house near Copenhagen and here bloom, already in early June, all the new glorious wild roses from China. Proudly aloft *Rosa Moyesii* rears its bloom-bedecked shoots above neighbouring *rugosa* roses: Blanc Double de Coubert and Frau Dagmar Hastrup. Its deep red blossoms stand out against a background of *Rosa oxyodon*'s pink flower-covered profusion, and of the many other species of wild rose which here conspire to form so beautiful a picture'.

ROSA HIGHDOWNENSIS is a near relation or a hybrid of *Rosa Moyesii*. It has large, single, pink carmine flowers and, in autumn, carries a wealth of large, red, bottle-shaped hips which gracefully, like tiny lamps, seem to illuminate its overhanging branches.

ROSA NEVADA is an extremely valuable new-comer to our park roses. The large, single, faintly pink blooms, which later turn pure white, and their golden-yellow pistils make a fascinating picture. The overhanging growth, the healthy foliage and the fact that this species is constantly in bloom should secure it a place in every garden or park. It is assumed to be a hybrid of *Rosa Moyesii*.

ROSA MULTIBRACTEATA is a near relation of the above. It has red flowers in panicles, though the numerous drooping orange-red, bottle-necked hips endow it throughout each succeeding winter with an added charm. Is probably not quite as hardy as the preceding species.

ROSA GALLICA (*Rosa provincialis;* the Provins rose) is, on the whole, a good vigorous and constant-flowering wild rose, suitable for planting in rose-beds. The blooms, large, dark-red and fragrant, are usually set singly, more rarely in threes. The shrub reaches about three feet in height and sends out a number of runners. Both *Rosa gallica*, as well as one of its near progeny: *Gallica splendena*, are good hardy garden plants. But it is not so much this that entitles *Rosa gallica* to so much fame as the fact that it is the mother of a very large family whose home was originally in Asia Minor and Southern Europe, and which now is spread over the entire globe. The Dutch began their work with the tulip in the seventeenth century. Later they continued their efforts in a similar way with the rose and especially with *Rosa gallica*. The French, encouraged by the Empress Josephine, whose rose garden at Malmaison was so famous, went on with the work late in the eighteenth and early in the nineteenth centuries; with the result that a profusion of new roses now appeared, of which the majority were of *gallica* extraction. Many of them were striped and vari-coloured, and if we are to believe the paintings of the day, and especially the fine illustrations in Miss Lawrance's beautiful hand-painted book (with ninety pictures of roses in the early nineteenth century), it would appear that there have been many beautiful specimens among them. But, as said before, all this perseverance has not been wasted, for, thanks to these tireless efforts, we have been able to fructify and further evolve, so that we too may be blessed with many and even more elegant and fragrant roses.

ROSA ALBA has long been known and written about. It was found growing wild in the Crimea and certain other places in Europe. It has always been described as a supposed hybrid between *Rosa canina* and *Rosa gallica*. In my opinion this does not coincide with the facts, for I have several times propagated it by sowing the seed, and I always found it constant and without change of any kind. *Rosa alba* is completely hardy. It forms a pretty, medium-high bush with light grey-green leaves and large, white, single flowers. A closely related form is *Rosa alba plena*. This was surely the plant introduced from Holland by Christian IV and planted in the Rosenburg gardens (Copenhagen), presumably as a hedge.

Rosa alba has yielded many delightful progeny, all in the 'old garden rose' style, healthy, strong and summer flowering only. We still know and grow quite generally, the delicate pink Maiden's Blush, the large-flowered densely-filled Rose Celestial and, possibly the finest of all the old roses, the beautifully formed, fragrant, delicate, darker towards the centre, Rose Queen of Denmark.

ROSA PENDULINA (*Rosa alpina*) adorns the mountain slopes of Central and Southern Europe. The growth is erect and its stems prettily red and shiny. The blooms are cherry-red and in winter there is a profusion of red hips.

The species is definitely hardy in Scandinavia; I have seen huge hoary old hedges of them in Stockholm (Sweden). It is of excellent effect when planted among other wild roses.

This rose is the mother of a now no longer cultivated garden rose, Boursault, which was widely grown in France round about 1820 and has through it by continued hybridising been instrumental in forming or, one might say, 'given of its blood' to form our present-day rose.

ROSA CENTIFOLIA (the cabbage rose) is the old hundred-leaved rose, called by many the Provence rose. It grows on its own roots around many a farm and fisherman's cottage in this country. It has been known and greatly esteemed from ancient times. From Greece and Asia Minor it spread westwards and northwards, and probably reached our gardens by about 1600. Many theories have been put forward as to its pedigree. Some suppose that *Rosa canina* or *Rosa gallica* were its progenitors, others have quite other ideas. As it is found wild in many districts of Southern Europe and Asia Minor, it has been assumed that it was a wild species, and incidentally, why shouldn't it be? There are so many wild plants that occasionally sport double-flowering individuals.

That many an old garden rose may run wild is obvious, especially as previously roses were planted on their own roots from runners. This is clearly exemplified in North America where, in the gardens planted by the first settlers on their now sometimes deserted farm sites, many of the good old now forgotten roses may still be found growing wild. They were brought from Europe and only planted when the immigrant pioneers reached their destination.

The centifolia rose is surely known to almost everybody. It is so easily distinguished by its numbers of typical green shoots and its small hooked prickles. The blooms are double, strongly perfumed and the light pink petals curl inwards. It is completely hardy and thrives on almost any kind of soil—though it is, of course, grateful for care and attention. From the strongly perfumed petals when mixed with lavender and kitchen salt a glorious potpurri may be made.

The moss-rose is assumed to be an offspring of the *centifolia* rose. This assumption is based on the fact that if moss-roses are grown in countries having a warm climate, like Italy and Spain, they will take on a *centifolia* appearance and lose their mossy covering.

ROSA CENTIFOLIA VAR. MUSCOSA (moss-rose). The moss-roses first appeared in England, where they were eagerly cultivated. William Paul, for instance, listed eighty-four different varieties in his catalogue and recommended them for common cultivation, even trained as espaliers and pillars. Treated in this way they sometimes reach a height of fifteen feet. The moss-rose is characterised by a mossy growth on leaf-stalks, flower-stalks and on sepals. As a rule they are vigorous plants with large leaves, hairy on the lower side, and with double fragrant blooms. Among the various types may be mentioned the common, red-cabbage rose; the rosy-pink *Cristata*, and the white Reine Blanche, etc. In addition to the ordinary moss-rose there are also certain types with a second display; among others, Blanche Moreau, the purple violet Eugenie Guinoisseau and the pink-shaded Salet.

ROSA DAMASCENA (damask rose) was formerly a much grown rose which is reported to have been brought to England from Damascus by Henry VII and Henry VIII's doctor. It is often found mentioned in sixteenth-century literature. It differs greatly from the *centifolia* roses in its more erect growth, its lighter bark and leaves, and in its habit of flowering with up to six or seven blooms together. The colour is deep red, but there are also certain pink, as well as white varieties.

The most widely known is the Kasanlik rose which is still grown in Bulgaria for the extraction of rose-petal oil.

But most famous of all is *variegata* the 'white and red rose' (pinky often striped with white) called 'York and Lancaster' famous in English history.

Otherwise Damascena has almost disappeared from our gardens and is now only found here and there in major rose collections; among these may be mentioned that at the Copenhagen Botanical Gardens, and the one at the Copenhagen Agricultural College. Its importance as one of the many old-time roses that have bequeathed something of their beauty, colouring and perfume to the hybrid perpetuals and hybrid teas should not be underestimated.

ROSA INDICA X GALLICA (the Bourbon rose). This family of roses is now practically forgotten, though it is still to be found, here and there, in old gardens. The well-known variety Hermosa is, however, still in cultivation.

Its origin is interesting and of considerable importance as this rose was the first gift from Chinese rose gardens to enrich our modern European varieties.

This happy union took place in 1817, on the island of Reunion, at that time called the Île de Bourbon, near the east coast of Africa. Here were to be found whole hedges of *Rosa chinensis* and *Rosa damascena*, and when a random seedling found here put forth, when only three months old, its first flowers, they proved to be of an entirely new type. It was brought to France and here proved of immense value in all later hybridisation experiments.

In 1951 the Danish gardener, D. T. Poulsen, released a cross between the Bourbon rose, Great Western, and the polyantha hybrid, Karen Poulsen. An English description of the new variety reads as follows: A large, robust bush some seven by seven feet in size with extremely dark, healthy and durable foliage, and carrying, in midsummer, on red stalks a wealth of pink Conrad F. Meyer-like, fragrant blooms, and bearing again in September, on strong firm shoots, prodigious clusters of flowers.

ROSA CHINENSIS (*Rosa indica;* the China or monthly rose). The Bengal Rose was introduced to Europe in 1768 and *Rosa chinensis semperflorens* (everflowering), the true Bengal Rose, presumably in 1789.

They were already old garden roses when we got them, and they much surprised rose cultivators of the day by blooming the whole summer through, a characteristic that had never before been witnessed. These two roses became the mothers of a whole series of new roses, called monthly roses. Varieties like Cramoisie Superieur, Fellenberg and Mme Laurette Messimy, are typical specimens. By continued cross-breeding we obtained our first Bourbon roses and hybrid perpetuals, and later—when the latter were crossed with tea roses—the hybrid teas. Also by crossing into *Rosa multiflora* and *Rosa moschata* new types of climbers and polyantha roses were evolved (see above).

Of the true origin of *Rosa chinensis* nothing is known. In 1789 Sir Joseph Baker introduced it to England and described it as a medium-tall, erect bush with green stems and with occasional typically hooked thorns. The leaves, with leaflets set in fives or sevens together, are smooth and glossy. The blooms are pink. The only wild specimen we know of the variety was found by Dr Henry in some ravines near Ichang (Central China). It was a tall, powerful, climbing bush equipped with occasional hooked thorns and, in contrast to the cultivated forms, the blooms were set singly and were of an unusually pale pink colour.

ROSA CHINENSIS SEMPERFLORENS, on the contrary, was of more slender growth, with only three of four divided, smooth, blue-bedewed leaves, and was, as the name leads us to suppose, seldom without flowers. It was introduced to England by Gilbert Slater. He was certainly a skilful and enthusiastic gardener, and was undoubtedly the *vera causa* why many valuable plants were cultivated in England. He distributed his knowledge and horticultural wealth to friends and acquaintances and it was not long before this rose became quite common in gardens in and near London.

ROSA ODORATA (*Rosa chinensis* (*indica fragrans*)). The Tea Rose is also a native of China. The first specimens came to Europe about 1809-10 and, like the preceding variety, were old cultivated forms. Fortune's Double Yellow was the first rose of that class to be tried.

The espalier roses, Gloire de Dijon and Reine Marie Antoinette are still generally known as good, hardy espalier varieties. And Maréchal Niel is still used for forcing purposes. Less well known are all the low delicate, finely built, profusely flowering forms, of which Mme Franciska Krüger, Maman Cochet and Bridesmaid are typical examples. The stronger and hardier hybrid teas are their offspring, produced by cross-breeding with the hybrid perpetuals.

This closes my chapter on wild roses and on our first cultivated varieties. A good deal more history has crept in, I fear, than I had originally intended. As an aid to my descriptions I have mainly consulted the *Genus Rosa* by Miss Wilmott, published in London in 1914.

I have myself cultivated all the roses, the tea roses and the Damask Rose, either in my private garden or in my nurseries and had, I thought, acquired a first-hand knowledge of their characteristics and behaviour; but the fatal winter of 1940-41 arrived and with its low, long-lasting temperatures made it evident that, if such winters were to become the rule in Denmark, our notions of hardiness would have to be radically revised. I know of no better advice to give, when winter is over, than to insert a remark in your catalogue recording its effects opposite each variety.

If, therefore, I venture later on in my book to mention supposedly hardy roses, my remarks must be taken to refer to our normal winter temperatures which, during the last ten years, have been exceptionally mild. In 1929 and in 1924, however, we experienced quite severe winters, though nothing like as cold or as long as those of 1940-41. Our experience then tends to be forgotten, or at any rate shelved, as of relative unimportance when one recollects the ten preceding summers with their prodigious wealth of bloom. After all, even if we missed seeing many a charming climber or wild rose blooming during the summers of 1940-41 we were fairly certain they would put out new shoots, and in coming summers flower as well as ever.

Even if some bad gaps should appear here and there in our rose-beds, it should not prove difficult to replant them. And then, maybe, we shall learn to give our roses some protecting cover the following winter and to heap up the earth as later on I

Picture

Spek's Yellow

suggest all rose-growers should do every year, however mild the winters, prevention being better than cure. However, doubtless we shall get lazy about it until another catastrophically long and severe winter comes along.

In 1947 we had another winter with long un-broken frost periods and no snow, so that though there were no exceptionally low temperatures, this had almost the same destructive effect as the winters of 1940-41. Again this time it was the large-flowered garden roses that suffered most, while the polyanthas came through better, even without any special protection.

It should be remembered that our wild roses possess more than purely æsthetic interest. In Norway and Sweden the use of hips for cooking purposes has always been general, but here in Denmark, like so many other things the old people knew and mastered, their use was forgotten, until the vital importance of vitamins was revealed, when our Dr Johanne Christiansen so warmly advocated the use of this fruit. Dr Christiansen has allowed me to quote what she writes on the hip in her *Rational Husbandry Cookery Book*, and, moreover, to draw the reader's attention to the many recipes for using it in making fruit juice, jam, sweet soups and jellies, and even wine.

'The life-giving energy embodied in the hip was well-known in ancient times. A thousand years ago the Salerno School wrote as follows: "We doctors are of opinion that the best cure for

C

haemorrhoids is to eat hips (without the skins or pips). Once taken, you will be vouchsafed relief—also from headaches, oral-catarrh, and gripe."

'In olden days powdered hips were used as a remedy for bleeding gums, and in Norway it was mixed with bread, for it was known that bleeding gums was a sure sign of scurvy. It is interesting to note how the old medical theories, as in so many cases, still hold good.

'An old doctor once told me that his good mother always had a pot of hip-jam handy for the sick villagers. Nothing livened them up so effectively as hips, she maintained. The dying can always enjoy hip-jam even when they cannot eat anything else! Her son came to consider it as something in the nature of "holy oil" and thought it a healthy example of the reliability of experience as opposed to much theoretical science and misconception.

'Hip-jam went out of use because it took too much time to clean the hips, but modern science has now restored them to favour.

'Not a single wild hip should be wasted; they are more valuable than oranges, and no garden should be without some specimens of the great *rugosa* rose. You may see them standing as a magnificent hedge round the memorial statue to Leonora Christina at Maribo. I was once down there in autumn and saw how all this quantity of vitamin C was allowed to rot untouched. If that wonderful woman had been alive today, she would certainly have made the inhabitants take better care.

'Wild-growing and garden-grown hips from Austrian copper roses, moss-roses, *Moyesii* and *Fargesii*, are also rich in vitamin C—as was proved by the valuable investigations undertaken by the State Council for Domestic Science—but they do not yield such a good crop as *Rosa rugosa*. Other garden varieties such as the large-flowered garden rose, and *Helanae*, are poor in vitamins.

'Unripe hips contain less vitamin C than ripe specimens, and dark or black over-ripe hips contain, as a rule, less than those just ripe. They should be plucked when they are still yellow or bright red.'

Dr Johanne Christiansen writes further that *Rosa rugosa* is the most fertile of all wild roses, and therefore she recommends it for general use, even though its milligramme content of vitamin C per 100 grammes fruit is considerably less than that of the *Rosa foetida bicolor* which has a content of 1340, and of the Moss-rose which contains 1470, while *Rosa rugosa* contains only 960 milligrammes.

I would suggest that there are numbers of wild roses whose vitamin content is sufficiently large to make it profitable to gather their fruit.

It was first and foremost our own wild dog-rose, as well as the *Rosa rubiginosa*, that our forefathers used with such beneficial effect, but other varieties, such as Dagmar Hastrup and Stella Polaris, both hybrids of *rugosa*, are, I suggest, more fertile and have better hips than the main stock.

The same holds good, of course, of the dog-rose varieties Mosvig and Skamling which are pure wild roses, while *Canina x Jacqueminot* which bears a prodigious harvest of large meaty hips should, I think, be examined for its vitamin C content.

The *rubiginosa* roses and all their garden variants are in appearance as wild as any dog-rose, and their hips so similar in every way that they, too, might be turned to account.

Among other wild roses with a wealth of bloom, there are *cinnamomea*, *oxyodon*, *humilis virginiana*, *carolina* and many others which, when discovered, should not be left to 'grace the desert air'.

CHAPTER TWO

The Choice and Planting of Roses

When to plant

AS WITH ALL DECIDUOUS PLANTS the best time for planting roses is when growth has ceased, either in October or November, or before growth recommences in April or May. In spring, however, it is possible to prolong the period for planting, as the roses that are for sale at this time have usually been dug up the previous autumn and held back at the nursery by burying them in a cool place. If needful, roses may well be planted in winter during a thaw or even in summer time, but in the latter case, only plants that have previously been planted in flower-pots, have taken root, and have formed a good root growth should be used, and they must be planted without damaging the roots. But, in reality, the best time for planting is in autumn or in early spring.

The right plants

The plants to choose should be one year old buddings (maidens), and preferably have been budded on briar stocks, such as *Rosa canina*, though, *Rosa multiflora* is suitable, and they may be either seedlings or cuttings of either. The latter are, however, best employed as stocks for polyanthas and climbers. Your plants should be healthy vigorous specimens with strong branches and good well-branched, undamaged roots.

It is very important that your plants be well protected from frost or drying out while being dug up and moved. Should it happen, however, that, in spite of all your care, their roots or crowns show signs of withering, do not despair, they are perhaps not entirely beyond remedy. Bury the whole plant in the ground at once, water it well, cover the earth with straw, sacking or compost, and put off planting a few days until the branches have regained their natural fresh green colour and gloss. Prepare a puddle of clay and earth, dip the plants in it, one at a time, and plant immediately. There are very few plants that are so sensitive to dessication as roses. Whether your plants have withered or not, it is always a wise precaution to first heel them in a prepared trench, then to dip them in the puddle and plant them as quickly and firmly as you can. And, whatever you do, don't let them lie out in the sun. Ten minutes or half an hour in a sharp, spring breeze is enough to give your roses a shock that will put them back considerably. In any case, it will take them longer to begin growing, and thus they cannot be expected to give a satisfactory result that year at least.

Where to plant

The ground should be prepared in good time before planting. The site and surroundings should be carefully considered, and the layout decided upon. The best place in the garden is never too good for roses. The site chosen should be an open situation, possibly adjoining a shelter-belt giving protection from northerly and westerly winds, with unhindered access to sun and air, but always so that they enjoy a sheltered position, and are not exposed to draught from between houses and hedges. It is not good, either, to plant under or near large trees, whose greedy and widely-searching roots quickly find the good earth in the rose-beds and steal water and nourishment from them. If this cannot be avoided, a deep trench should be dug between the rose-beds and the tree or trees in question; sever all tree roots, stand some tarred felt on edge in the trench and stamp the earth firmly up against it. In this way it is possible to keep the tree roots away from the rose-beds for several years.

Conifers or conifer hedges are not such dangerous neighbours as elm, chestnut, beech, walnut and other large trees.

The best soil

Ordinary good, healthy soil, preferably with good friable mould, or sandy clay as a foundation, is best for roses. They may, however, thrive well also both in clayey or sandy soil, provided, of course, that the former is not too moist and the latter not plain shore-sand, or is not too dry. It may sometimes be necessary to improve the soil, e.g. near new buildings where the subsoil has been shot out (when the ground was dug out for the house foundations), over the place where the roses are to stand, or if, when levelling the garden, some or all of the good upper soil was dug up and removed elsewhere. In such cases the unsuitable soil should be dug away a couple of spits in depth and replaced by healthy, clayey loam. It may also be necessary, if the foundations are too wet or cold, to drain away the subsoil water, and to put in a layer of coarse rubble at the bottom of the drain. The exact opposite is the case if the soil is too light and sandy. In this case it may be necessary to mix it with clayey loam, or to improve it by adding coarse peat-litter or possibly some old farmyard manure.

And, finally, there is the third possibility that the prospective planting place consists of dank marshy soil. It is seldom that the site for a house or garden is chosen as specially good for roses. It will therefore often be necessary to carry out draining and digging operations and to add enough lime to bring the pH reaction figure up to five or six. Should there be any doubt as to the amount of lime in the soil, a sample may be sent in for examination to any County Agricultural Service.

In former days people were firmly convinced that roses were lime-loving plants, and all that was necessary to improve their growth and vigour, they thought, was to pile on heaps of lime. This, we now know, is quite wrong. One may often find roses thriving uncommonly well on comparatively lime-free soil.

New soil is nearly always advisable when re-planting old rose-beds with new roses, or in old urban gardens containing dank, over-manured soil.

Occasionally fresh new soil may be obtained at a reasonable figure through a haulage-contractor in the suburbs. Fresh soil and fresh air are two good allies if one wishes to grow good, healthy roses.

In any case, in trying to make a vigorous and flourishing rose-bed it is always a good precaution to dig the plot to a depth of two spits. That is to say the top spit is dug away first together with the loose earth. Next we dig over, one spit deep, the second layer at the bottom of the trench, at the same time mixing in a suitable amount of old manure and peat-litter. We now return the upper prepared layer, and, finally, allow the earth to settle properly before beginning planting operations. The old assumption that it was good to put in a layer of cow or other strong manure at the bottom of the trench is now known to be erroneous, for such manures form too much carbon dioxide in the soil and give the roses a feeble, yellow appearance.

When to plant

It is of course best to plant your roses as soon as they come. It is always better to plant in the afternoon or towards evening, and do take care that the plants are given no chance of drying out, as mentioned above.

Examine each specimen before you plant it, cut

out any damaged branches or roots and prune back
the head, in autumn to about a foot, and in spring
to about five inches. The roots should be trimmed
lightly—it is better to plant a rose with its roots
trimmed back than to bend them round in the
planting hole with the ends of the roots sticking
upwards. The soil should be easily workable,
being neither too dry nor too wet. The planting-
hole should be sufficiently large for there to be
plenty of room to spread out the roots in a natural
way. Hold the bush so deep, while planting, that
the graft-union is about two and a half inches
below the surface; shake the plant while the earth
is being filled in around it, and then lift it sufficiently to bring the graft-union about one to one-
and-a-half inches below the surface level of the
ground. Press down the earth firmly. Far more
roses die from loose planting than from any other
cause! Before the remaining soil is filled in, the
new plants should be given a good watering.

The graft-union in a rose is the place on the
neck of the root from which the branches sprout,
and where there is usually a slight swelling.
Either in autumn, or spring, it is advisable to heap
up the earth round this union and the lower
branches, partly to protect them from drying out
and partly from frost. And please don't try to
remove it before you are well into the month of
March when the danger of further night frosts is
over, or, better still, wait till the newly planted
bushes have begun sprouting new shoots.

The distance between plants should vary between one and one and a half feet according to the size and growth of individual plants, though here I refer solely to such varieties as are planted in beds and borders.

Manuring new-planted roses is not necessary if they are planted in good nourishing soil, and overdone, it may even be harmful. All artificial manures should be anathema, but a little well decayed farmyard manure may be mixed in, particularly if the soil is light and sandy. Only when the roses have grown new roots and leaves and have absorbed all the nourishment in the earth around them is it time to give new supplies. I shall return to this point later.

Planting standards

Standard roses are less popular in our Danish gardens nowadays, and still less often found planted in the right way, being nearly always planted singly, and never in groups, which is a far more attractive lay-out, and of greater decorative effect. Planted in groups the mutual distance between plants should be from one foot eight inches to two feet three inches. The best time to plant is in spring.

The stocks used for budding standards should be either *Rosa canina* or its variety *Rosa canina x General Jacqueminot*.

The procedure for planting standards is the same as that for half or quarter standards, i.e. first by making large planting holes into which the stake is driven to which the rose will be tied (the stake should be long enough to reach up through the head of the plant), next by shaking the earth well in among the root fibres and then by treading the earth firm, after having given a thorough watering, etc. As the grafted head of a standard rose springs from the top of a long stem, it is impossible to cover it with earth except by bending the head down, and heaping the earth over it. This can be done, of course, but the plant should be released and not re-tied to the stake until the head has shown signs of sprouting. (But this method of winter protection is not practical in England on account of the milder climate.)

A better plan is to tie the rose to the stake immediately after planting, and then to tie damp moss, grass, peat-litter, etc., among the branches of the head and around the graft-union and thereafter keeping this protective covering moist until the rose-tree is growing well when it may be removed. (*vide* section on Treatment of Dwarf Roses.)

Climbers, ramblers, wild and bush roses are all planted in the same way as above, but should be pruned back less drastically. Should the climbers be provided with long stems, and a display of flowers be desired the first summer, the long stems may be laid along the ground and covered up until mild weather sets in and growth has begun, and only then tie them up to their pergola or hedge.

CHAPTER THREE

Cultivation of Roses

LET US SUPPOSE that our roses have come undamaged and safely through the winter, and begin
when the danger of severe night-frosts is usually
over, about the tenth of April (or the middle of
March in England), by removing their protective
covering. It will then be seen that they are already
swelling into new activity. Tender shoots will be
observed peeping out, and we see the main reason
for not removing their protective covering too
soon.

After having removed all the loose material that
was used for winter protection, and before the
earth heaped up round our plants is levelled down,
the first supplies of manure may be given.

First supply of manure

During their first spring roses planted the previous autumn should either be given no manure at
all or at most very little. The best manure for
roses is old, well decayed, farm manure. This may
be plentifully supplied without doing much harm,
but artificial manures should be used only with
great circumspection.

If the earth is otherwise well provided with
nourishing elements, we can content ourselves with
some kind of nitrogenous manure, either nitrate

of Calcium Ca $(NO_3)_2$, or, on chalky ground, sulphate of ammonia $(NH_4)_2SO_4$. Nitrogenous manures are always quick-acting and of rather one-sided effect. This will soon be evident in the stronger growth and larger-sized, dark-green foliage. Moreover, the rose-trees will be more active in root and head, but as the effect of these manuring remedies is but short-lived, further supplies of a more universal character should be given later on in summertime.

It is better to give a more balanced manure at once, and one which, in addition to nitrogen, also contains potash and superphosphate. There are several ready-mixed manures of this kind on the market, such as Nitrophoska or D.T. Poulsen's mixed manure, or, if so preferred, one can make one's own manure by mixing equal parts of sulphate of ammonia, superphosphate and sulphate of potash. Should these manuring mediums be difficult to obtain, one can make-do with bonemeal and hoof and horn shavings; the latter two should, however, be strewn in autumn, as they dissolve rather slowly.

How much to use depends on whether it is a question of young bushes with only a small head and root which are thus incapable of absorbing and utilising much at a time, or whether they are older bushes that fill the bed with their heads and roots, and which are therefore able to consume larger amounts at once.

I would propose using roughly 2 lb. per 100 sq. ft. of the pure nitrogen manure for the weaker plants and 4 lb. for the larger ones, while at least double the amount may be used of the mixed manure.

The soil heaped up round the rose bushes in autumn is now levelled down over the manure, and pruning operations can begin. Should the rose-beds be so large that one cannot prune the roses without trampling on them, a few boards to step on may be laid between the bushes until pruning operations are over.

Pruning

How to prune roses may be learnt by the merest novice. The first step to visualise is how the roses are to develop next summer, whether long-stalked blooms are wanted for indoor decoration or for exhibition purposes; one must get to know the character and behaviour of the various sorts before pruning them, whether they are thickly branched, small-flowered climbers or ramblers, suitable for grouping, or tall, erect, large-flowered kinds. They may be hardy, floriferous varieties like Betty Prior and Kirsten Poulsen and be planted to make tall bushes (vide section on Continuous-flowering varieties for Rose-beds), and one must, of course, know the best pruning method for the object in view. All this will be dealt with in a later section.

Let us deal, first of all, with garden roses planted in beds or borders.

The actual pruning should be carried out with

a sharply ground secateur to avoid the possibility
of crushing the wood; the cuts, which should be
smooth and slanting, should be made above a well-
developed bud, and always end with the upper lip
of the cut slightly above the bud.

Roses planted in autumn should be cut back to
two or three buds above ground level. All small,
thin or damaged twigs should be removed entirely.
With such plants it is sufficient to start them with
only three or four shoots.

Among other types, hybrid perpetuals should be
allowed to retain more wood than hybrid teas for,
by cutting back too severely, one robs them of a
major part of their blooming capacity.

Firstly, begin by removing the thinnest branches
as well as branches that are too old; then reduce
the remaining branches to four, or possibly six,
according to the amount of space they are to occupy
and shorten them down to one foot above ground
level. Vigorous sorts, like Hugh Dickson, may well
retain up to two feet of their stem length.

Hybrid teas should be pruned in a similar man-
ner to hybrid perpetuals, but, if an abundant display of flower is desired the first year, they should
be cut down to six or eight inches above ground
level.

By cutting the specially large-flowered sorts
down to only a few buds above ground the plant
is induced to give its first display about a week
later than would otherwise be the case, as well as
to produce longer stalks and larger blooms without

President Herbert Hoover

Sun Dance

the rose-beds being less well filled or poorer in flower.

Polyantha roses and hybrid polyanthas are pruned in essentially the same way as hybrid teas, though preferably rather short than long.

All cuttings should be carefully collected and burnt.

The severe cold experienced during the 1939-40 winter was the cause of a wholesale freezing back of practically all kinds of rose groups, and was a weighty argument in favour of those who advocate short pruning: everyone was amazed at the exuberance and vigour the surviving roses later exhibited, due possibly to the fact that all old and infected wood had had to be removed right down to the ground. It also proved the necessity of deep planting, and the importance of heaping up the ground as a protection from frost.

That so many roses froze to death was due, I think, solely to the fact that they were planted too high, or that the earth around them had sunk too low without being supplemented with new supplies.

I hasten to add, however, that many nurserymen hold the opposite opinion, viz. to cut back as little as possible, merely thinning out and trimming back to vigorous buds. They maintain that pruning too severely weakens the rose-tree's roots and that equally large and beautiful roses may be obtained with almost no pruning at all.

This is only possible, of course, after mild winters with little or no damage from frost, and

D

only then to a certain degree. But naturally the method may be supplemented by summer pruning and thinning out.

These breast-high, flower-bedecked rose bushes may be an enchanting sight, but they require more room and sometimes repeated tying up.

Should a long period of drought set in, as is often the case in April or May, it may be necessary towards the end of May or in early June, to give the rose-beds a good watering, or indeed several. The manure put in should be completely dissolved, if it is to be of assistance in boosting the rose-tree's first display.

Spraying and dusting

With due regard to expected attacks, during the approaching summer, of the worst enemies of the rose, viz. mildew and black spot and, in order to kill disease-spores that have survived the winter, our plants should now be given their first and thorough spraying, during which plants and the ground around them should both be effectively sprayed. For this purpose a 10% solution of Bordeaux mixture should be made according to the maker's instructions if a ready-mixed product is used.

It is very seldom that roses are attacked by disease before their first display, which usually opens up towards the close of June, but none the less it may be wise to take due precaution.

A good insecticide that is quite harmless to

humans and warm-blooded animals, which I can, from personal experience, warmly recommend, is Midox which prevents the unpleasantness and risk of using the extremely poisonous sprays that have been the cause of numbers of unfortunate accidents among children and domestic animals.

Midox may be used, as often as one cares, the moment any green-fly, caterpillars or cicada appear on leaves or branches, or thrips in the flowers.

In order to simplify and lighten work in the garden, I would recommend Bordeaux powder for black spot, and sulphur powder for mildew. Some handy small powder blowers can now be obtained in the shops with which dusting can be carried out quickly and without any drawbacks. It is best to dust one's plants in early morning or late evening on a quiet day, and this should be repeated several times during the summer—more often in rainy periods than in dry—and always after rain, which swills off the powder from former dustings.

Thinning out

By the end of May or early in June the rose-beds should be the picture of health and vitality, and they should have put forth a wealth of young shoots, often so many that if the plant is allowed to develop all the blooms it has set, it will spend itself on this first display and therefore take longer than necessary to yield another. A group of Hybrid perpetuals should bloom the whole summer through, and this is not difficult to ensure if one thins out in good time and allows only the healthiest and most vigorous stems to bloom.

The remaining weaker shoots, usually comprising about half the plant, should be pinched back just above the first well-developed leaf. These pinched shoots will quickly develop, and will stand ready with new buds when the first blooming is over.

The shoots that have finished flowering should then also be pruned back.

It is not enough just to pinch off the faded blooms, the shoots must be cut right back to the first well-developed leaf. In this way one's rose-bushes may be kept continuously in bloom; they will keep their fresh, healthy appearance and will be better able to resist the attacks of insects and disease. It is a foregone conclusion that all faded flowers and leaves should be continually removed and the soil around the plants kept loose.

In very warm and dry summers a good deal of watering and loosening of the earth may be dispensed with by spreading grass cuttings from the lawns or a layer of coarse peat-litter among one's rose-bushes.

Second supply of manure

In July, after the first display is over, a second supply of manure should be given. This, like the first supply, should consist of Poulsen's mixed fertiliser, Nitrophoska, or the above-mentioned home-made mixture, followed by a thorough watering, loosening of the soil and possibly soil coverage, as described before.

During the growing stage, roses are, of course, grateful for all kinds of manure including animal droppings. Many owners of gardens keep poultry and/or pigeons. Both kinds are extremely quick-acting, nourishing manures which should be dissolved in water and not used in a too concentrated solution. They should be given after the ground has previously been thoroughly watered. A sackful of hoof and horn shavings soaked in a tub of water may also be equally effective and may be used, gradually as the shavings dissolve, in the same way and in not too powerful doses.

The newly-planted roses, whether planted in autumn or in spring, will now be able to stand manuring, as it may be assumed that by now they will be fully established and will have grown good new roots and a well developed head.

Roses planted in spring

In the section on spring-planting we recommend that the soil should be heaped up round the plants, left there until growth had begun, and only removed on a mild day when the air was sufficiently moist.

In spite of every care taken when planting, there may still be a few backward plants which sprout but slowly and feebly, and which produce only few and short shoots. Such plants should not be allowed to flower at once; all flower buds should be pinched off. An astonishing improvement will then quickly be noticed; all the power that should have been used for producing flowers will now be used to assist the many rapidly sprouting shoots.

Summer runs its course and our roses still continue to flower. All through July, August, September, October and sometimes even till far into November, one's rose-beds may be a never-ending joy. But never-ending care and attention is always necessary. The first display in June is almost a certainty, but without due care that will be the only one. It will get hot, the soil cracks with the heat, mildew and black spot set in, the leaves fall off and, for the rest of the summer but a few miserable blooms at the ends of almost leafless twigs are all that is to be seen. And that is why, in the above, I have given such minute directions for cultivation. If these suggestions are followed, all talk of special diseases and insect pests will be superfluous. For, after all, both are due solely to wrong methods of cultivation.

Mildew, Black Spot and Rose Rust

In the above directions given for tending roses I have repeatedly mentioned the two worst enemies of the garden rose, mildew and black spot, and have suggested means of mastering their attacks, special weight being laid on thoroughly rational methods of cultivation.

Mildew is the more notorious of the two diseases. The spores that have hibernated in the rose-tree's lateral buds, and have survived the preceding winter, may cause quite early attacks. These may be quickly recognised in the crippled shoots covered with a white mealy powder that make their appearance when the buds burst. Such shoots as well as affected leaves must be removed immediately and burnt.

It is mainly on account of these surviving spores that the first vigorous spraying with a 10% solution of sulphurated lime is so necessary.

As is the case with mildew, the spores of the Black Spot disease hibernate in last year's infected branches, in fallen leaves and even in the soil itself. The disease seldom appears until after the first display, late in July or early in August, and then only on the lowest, densest and oldest leaves while the young leaves and plants in vigorous growth are seldom so susceptible. The pathological picture of the disease is black spots, first small, then growing gradually in size and spreading almost all over leaf and shoot. All affected leaves and shoots should be carefully removed the moment the disease is discovered, and the bush at once dusted.

In combating this disease it is very important that all leaves, shed flowers and infected shoots be carefully removed from rose-bushes and rose-beds every autumn before they are covered up for winter. This procedure in conjunction with effective summer hygiene, will keep your plants healthy and well.

That my observations seem to be correct is borne out by what has been found in France and England. A French amateur, for instance, writes that the first spraying immediately after pruning is the most important, as I have suggested; he also recommends a 2% solution of Bordeaux mixture similar to that used for spraying fruit trees. Personally I have substituted powder for this spray in order to avoid spotting the foliage. He is also a warm advocate of using the mixed manure which, after long experience, I, too, found so good and have duly recommended, viz. equal parts of sulphate of ammonia, superphosphate and sulphate of potassium K_2SO_4 with a slightly larger proportion of the latter; as he found that this ingredient invigorates the foliage and makes it better proof against attacks of mildew, black spot and rust. As good preventive measures, English nurserymen also warmly recommend the soil to be kept loosened between plants; to avoid trampling on it; and to avoid the necessity of doing so by never making one's rose-beds or borders larger than can be reached from all sides; and finally, to cover the soil in one's rose-beds with the grass cuttings from one's lawns.

Rose Rust, so easily recognised by the small rust-red blotches on the lower surface of the leaves, is a disease for which some roses seem to have a natural or inherited disposition. They are often infected from without by air-borne spores or by spores from suckers springing from the base of the stock on which the garden rose was budded. The first attack is often observed as spore-filled, orange-coloured swellings on the young shoots. These may be effectively dealt with by breaking off and burning them, and then powdering the plant as described above. It is strongly recommended all summer through, and especially after the first display, to keep a sharp lookout for the first attacks of mildew and black spot; for, by carefully plucking off the first leaves and shoots that show signs of attack, and by following this up by powdering with Bordeaux mixture, the attacks may be largely checked.

Should one's plants seem to have stopped growing, they may be stimulated by supplies of sulphate of ammonia or nitrophoska followed up by a good watering.

'Suckers' is the name given to the vigorous shoots springing from under or around the place on the root where the rose was budded. They must be cut away right back to their starting point. If this is not done they will grow again with redoubled vigour. They are easily distinguished from the budded part of the rose bush by their nine or eleven leaflets, and must not be mistaken for the basal shoots sprouting later in summer from the budded part of the root. The latter are usually of a reddish colour, have larger leaves and thorns and quickly start quite large-scale inflorescence.

Insect pests

Most of the pests that attack roses, as mentioned above, are comparatively easy to control by using the non-poisonous insecticide Midox. But there is a species of saw-fly grub that lives inside the juicy young shoots, feeding on the pith, that gives us quite a lot of trouble. There is, indeed, only one effective remedy, viz. to find the grubs and pinch them to death.

The tiny red spider *Tetranychus telarius* lives on the lower sides of the leaves, and in dry warm summers often in considerable numbers, where it sucks the sap from the leaves, so that they turn grey and droop in a sickly way. The only thing to be done in this case is to spray plentifully and energetically with Midox, mostly on the lower sides of the leaves. Several vigorous sprayings with cold water straight from the tap, and preferably in the evening, may check the red spiders' development but will hardly prove fatal.

A less conspicuous insect is the thrips, but in warm summers it, too, may be very troublesome. It is a very tiny, almost invisible creature that starts life in the rose while the latter is still only in bud. By gorging itself on the young petals it causes their malformation, hampers their growth, and gives them a brown edging. Quite often, it is the Ophelia varieties and Ellen Poulsen, that suffer first.

The above-mentioned insecticides may well have a somewhat restrictive effect, but as the insect eats more than sucks, the most effective remedy is to poison its food; and, as the thrips has a sweet-tooth, it is advisable to use Paris green dissolved in water to which has been added a sugar solution, and spray the mixture direct on to flowers and buds. But be careful with the Paris green. It contains a dangerous arsenic compound!

In November the rose season is over and it is time to think of winter. In this connection, I cannot help wondering how all those lukewarm rose-enthusiasts who so consistently fail to protect their roses in winter feel, after the severe winters we have been having lately. My experience is that it is always wiser to earth up one's roses, if not always on account of winter's chill blast, at least on account of spring sunshine and night frosts, which occasionally may prove more dangerous than the constant cold of real winter.

The hardiness of a plant must be judged in relation to the country and the climatic zone in which it is grown, also in relation to the nature of the soil; for many plants, including roses, have proved more immune to frost on high-lying, light sandy soil than on a low-lying clay soil.

Moreover, no winter need be specially severe to kill our garden roses, which all have in them a strain of the not absolutely hardy tea-rose blood.

Changeable weather, night frost, sun and a dessicating wind even in late March or early April may prove the cause of many a rose's demise and that although it may have weathered the first part of the winter with flying colours.

The best covering is soil heaped up among the branches of the rose. It should be drawn up over the rose with a hoe, never with a spade, for the latter implement may easily go too deep, thus laying bare the roots and opening up an easy path for Brother Frost to bite his way even deeper into the earth.

There are two implements that should never be used in a rose-bed, and, incidentally, in any other flower-bed either. One is a spade and the other a Dutch hoe. A spade only serves to break off branches and sever useful roots, and in the perennial border it roots out the choicest plants neck and crop; while a Dutch hoe wounds the plants and only leaves the earth hard and scaly. With a small hoe or a digging fork the earth is easily loosened to the right depth and weeds are removed without trouble.

After the earth has been heaped up over the plant it may be covered with a light layer of dry leaves or straw and finally with a light layer of spruce twigs, but not too thick. No kind of material of a slimy nature should be used or any that may cause rot among the rose branches.

Standards should be well wrapped up in airtight parchment, which should be tied securely above and below the 'head' and, for the sake of appearance the bags and stems may be covered with spruce.*

It is not wise to uncover one's roses before early April (Mid-March in England), not even though a few brilliantly fine spring days in March may tempt one to renewed activity in the garden. It is wiser far to direct your surplus energy to the kitchen-garden where you may sow your early vegetables, or sweet peas, but do leave your roses in peace!

Standards should be pruned in much the same way as dwarfs, only giving more attention to form than to lengthy or close pruning.

Ramblers, tending and pruning

In the section on how to plant roses I mentioned briefly the way to plant climbers and ramblers. Actually they do not require much attention the first two years, over and above keeping them properly tied up. A gentle trimming, possibly some spraying for mildew and a little pruning are all that is necessary, coupled with the necessary removal in spring of withered, frozen, and damaged branches. The pruning of climbers and ramblers can best be compared with the method employed with raspberries and blackberries. Climbers need the first two years to grow and fully occupy the space allotted to them. In the third

* In England these precautions are very seldom necessary. When the exceptional winter does come, however, the English amateur rose-grower may well wish he had taken Mr Poulsen's advice.

year, however, the pergola, post, wall space or fence to which they are attached will be covered with flowering shoots, and thus a number of these shoots, which bloom so profusely during the third summer, will be rendered superfluous later on by the numerous new shoots that continually spring from the base.

The pruning method to be employed in the third and following years should therefore be as follows:

Sometime in early August when flowering is over operations should begin. Our main concern is carefully to select and tie up the new shoots now and in such a way that they will develop in full sunshine and gain such maturity and vigour during the last remaining summer months, that they will again provide the same beauty and the same wealth of bloom as they did in the summer just over—or, if possible, even better.

And now to work: First cut back all branches that have finished flowering so that only three leaves remain intact on each. Next cut right away all old branchings for which there is no room, and in their place tie up the best and most vigorous stems that spring from the base of the plant—as many as you can find room for; the rest must be cut out entirely. Those who know the charming pergola of roses at Fredensborg Park will probably have admired its beautifully bound up, flower-bedecked arches. Here, the various ramblers' shoots are renewed every year according to the above recipe.

This pruning method is best employed with ramblers of the Dorothy Perkins type, that is to say, with varieties that are inclined to renew themselves with numerous, vigorous new shoots from the base. Even among these, however, there are exceptions, as some varieties do not flower willingly from first year's young wood. Among these are Aglaia, Dr W. van Fleet, New Dawn, Paul's Scarlet Climber, as well as all the sorts listed under espalier roses.

All perpetual flowering climbers, climbing types of large flowered roses and all small flowered cluster roses must be treated as soon as possible in the same way as strong-growing bush roses; that is to say, thinned, trimmed and bound up when they are pruned in spring. They flower all summer through and may be trimmed while flowering. They will not reach the height of real climbers but they are well suited for planting near low fences or as solitary bushes.

It is only natural that such vigorous plants need plenty of water and nourishment if they are to produce new shoots every year and a similar wealth of bloom. So water them well and give them plenty of food. Their roots search farther afield for nourishment than do those of dwarf types, but even so, there will come a day when growth and flowering will decline, usually in the third or fourth year. The manure recommended for dwarf garden roses is equally good for ramblers or climbers. Two or three handfuls for each plant will be about right, just as the same spraying and dusting methods may be used for both. Ramblers are in no wise different from other garden plants; the better they are fed in the right way the more immune do they become to attacks of disease, and the greater their profusion of bloom, and the better the flowers will they produce.

Climbers against a wall

It is for the reasons given above that climbers planted against a wall often do not prosper, and that they are generally covered with mildew. They can seek out their water and nourishment to one side only, and that often a hard-trampled garden path.

However, there is nothing to prevent one's raking the gravel aside in early spring; spreading artificial manure, hoeing it lightly in; giving it a good watering and then replacing the gravel.

It is also quite a good idea to bury a drain-pipe standing upright on coarse cinders a short distance from any plant and water the subsoil through it all summer, or a supply of liquid manure might be given.

Espalier roses

To be on the right side, one should avoid planting any climber with a tendency to mildew against a wall. The varieties best suited for this position are the climbing teas, climbing hybrid teas, certain perpetuals like Charles Bonnet, and all climbing noisette roses like William Allen Richardson, Rêve d'Or, etc. And among the real climbers only the large flowered sorts including, perhaps, Dr van Fleet and New Dawn. Pruning these climbers, or espalier roses as they are sometimes called, should be carried out quite differently to that recommended for the varieties first described: the job should preferably be done in spring, being merely a question of trimming the lateral shoots, removing damaged branches and tying up young shoots in their proper place.

Summer pruning consists of trimming and tying up as many shoots from the base or new lateral shoots from the woody stems as there may be room for. The remainder should be cut out completely.

The protection of climbers and ramblers in winter is a more troublesome task. The best method, perhaps, is to wrap them up in a thick covering of spruce twigs. Or one may detach them from their pergola or fence, lay the long pliable stems along the ground, heap them over with earth or spruce, and hope that the coming winter's snow will spread a sufficiently protective covering over them. In northern Sweden, in Norway and in Finland they always cover up their ramblers or climbers in one of these ways. In this country, however, we hardly ever trouble to cover them up, and that is why our roses are so often frozen down during severe winters, at least once every fifth or possibly every tenth year. Fortunately, most of them usually recover fairly quickly.

E

Among the perpetual flowering climbers there is one called Blaze which is a sport of Paul's Scarlet Climber, and another New Dawn that is a sport of Dr van Fleet. Their perpetual character is thus not original but has developed through mutation, and this being so, every effort must be made to fix it by carefully choosing one's propagating material at the nursery.

Planted out as a hedge or espalier it will quickly lose its everlasting character if, through wrong pruning in summer after the first display, the de-flowered shoots are cut back too drastically. Only the outer tip where the bloom has withered should be trimmed. It is just these flower buds which will be the ones to continue the display if they are spared.

Pruning and tending wild roses

Pruning and tending wild roses and hardy summer flowering bush roses is a somewhat less arduous task. Here our object is to retain the best features of individual form of growth. This is best managed by lightly thinning out, removing old and dead branches, and, possibly, if the rose bush has grown too large by reducing it to reasonable proportions.

This should be done after the display is over, as all these roses flower only once.

Among the hardy bush roses there are a number of varieties with large well-filled flowers. There are the centifolia roses, the moss-roses, sorts like

Maiden's Blush, Cellini, Celestial, Queen of Denmark, Coupe d'Hébé and others, whose growth is not so exceptionally beautiful or characteristic that their form need be given undue consideration. On the contrary it may be necessary by appropriate pruning to give the bushes a better form; just as it may be necessary to cut back some of the young shoots, partly to get larger and better flowers and partly to prevent the heavy profusion of bloom from weighing the branches down to the ground. And even then it may be necessary to support them on stakes during the display.

CHAPTER FOUR

How to grow Roses in Flower-Pots for indoor cultivation, for the Winter-Garden or Hot-House, and Names of suitable Varieties

IN OLDEN DAYS this was a very popular pastime, and one still known and much favoured today among our northern neighbours, as well as in the Faeroes, in Iceland and Greenland, where it is, in fact, the only known way of growing roses at all; for out-of-doors it is, of course, impossible.

All hybrid-teas and polyanthas are well suited for this purpose as they are all free-flowering and perpetual. The choice of varieties may be left to individual taste, though I would strongly recommend novices to stick to the easier sorts like: Ellen and Grethe Poulsen, Grüss an Aachen, Ophelia, Mme Butterfly and Roselandia, as well as the charming deep-red Etoile de Hollande.

The procedure is as follows: In October or November, vigorous, well-branched specimens are planted in six-inch flower-pots in a soil consisting mainly of fresh heavy loam mixed with a little hot-bed manure, peat-litter and coarse grit. First a crock is put in the bottom of the pot to cover the hole, then a handful of earth, and then the plant itself, the roots and branches of which have already been suitably pruned in readiness. More soil is filled in, taking care that it is shaken well in among the roots, and that the budded union is not higher than the top edge of the flower-pot. The remaining soil is now filled in till it covers the roots properly, and, with three or four useful jolts against the table-top one tries to shake the earth together as firmly as possible. Lastly, with one's thumbs or some blunt instrument, the earth is pressed more firmly still. The plant should now be firmly seated and the soil should fill the pot to within half an inch of the rim. The proper soil mixture is a good rich loam from a kitchen garden or field mixed with 1/5 coarse grit and 1/5 granulated peat.

The pots containing the roses are now buried out-of-doors or stored in a frost-proof cellar. In the first case the soil should be heaped up among the branches and the heap covered with spruce twigs. The following spring the pots, spaced slightly apart, are bedded out and watered regularly, first with plain water and, later on, with liquid manure or fertiliser. Before next winter sets in they are taken in and stored in a frost-proof cellar.

Round about the new year the plants should be pruned, the small, weaker twigs being cut entirely, and, in forming the new rose, the stronger branches should be reduced to half their length, just above a healthy outward-turned bud. The plant is now carefully de-potted, taking care not to damage the roots, the crock at the bottom of the pot is re-arranged to give better and easier drainage, and the top inch of earth covering the roots when in the pot is removed. The remaining root-filled ball is now returned to the pot and the latter refilled to the top with a mixture consisting of three parts of soil and one part of hoof and horn powder, the whole mass being pressed firmly together and well watered.

Having got so far, there is really nothing to prevent our beginning forcing operations at once, but it is wiser to wait until both crown and roots show unmistakable signs of new growth. A hot-house or a conservatory is, of course, the best and only right place for forcing roses. But a good window, preferably one of the large, specially light picture windows to be found in modern houses, will, however, do; and may be made to give excellent results. The main feature necessary to ensure the well-being of our roses is that the room is not too hot and that there is no direct radiation from the heating-unit.

The plants should be watered in a proper and sensible way, that is to say, they must be allowed to almost dry out between each watering, and should be given a plentiful supply of water each time. The more leaves they have and the nearer they get to the flowering stage the more water they need.

As regards nourishment they will have sufficient, in the slowly decomposing hoof and horn shavings, to carry them over the first and second flowering. After the first display they should be slightly cut back. Should they become infected with green-fly or at the first sign of mildew the plants can be taken into the bathroom and given a thorough spraying with Midox solution. The right strength to use is printed on the label.

One or two thorough weekly sprayings with cold water will serve to keep the plants clean and free from Red Spider. These tiny creatures specially attack roses that are cultivated under glass and most of all when they stand near a radiator or in too dry air. Roses grown in flower-pots may grow to a ripe old age, but they must be put out in the garden every summer. The pot should be buried in a bed and they must be tended and looked after as carefully as they were during their first year. Every year, before forcing begins, they must be given the above-mentioned soil renewal including the hoof and horn powder, and if properly cared for will thrive winter after winter in the same flower-pot for as much as eight or ten years.

Garden owners who possess a hot-house or conservatory, even without a heating unit, may derive considerable pleasure from cultivating roses. Protected by the protective glass roof, the roses will thrive and develop freely and well, and will, moreover, stand up to no little frost. In winter they should be kept dry and not be pruned before well into March (February in England), when growth recommences. On warm sunny days, in winter, they should be aired occasionally.

Such rose bushes will give their owner many a

happy hour and plenty of healthy exercise, not to mention many exceptionally beautiful flowers into the bargain.

The soil should be prepared in the same way as in the open and that regardless of whether the roses are planted in the border or whether in beds shored up with concrete or brick in the hot-house. The roses should be planted in October-November and pruned and heaped up with soil. Never use artificial fertilisers or other kinds of strong manure immediately, but you need not hesitate to use them when the rose bushes have become fully established.

Repeated vigorous sprayings with cold water straight from the tap, and mostly on the lower sides of the leaves, are the best remedy against Red Spider. Avoid planting varieties disposed to mildew.

Now this is a case where I feel justified in recommending the dangerous smoke-remedy, Bladan (HETP or TEPP), which is now on sale. It is fatal to all green-fly, red spider, woolly aphis, etc. Use the smoke only in quiet weather and in the evening. Make sure the hot-house is air-tight and locked, and do not forget to thoroughly air the hot-house the following day.

If you are not keen on using this remedy, spray your roses with Midox. Directions for use are given on the package.

In airing your hot-house open the windows on the lee side, and if the sun is too hot, draw the blinds, otherwise the leaves of many of your plants may be scorched by the strong spring sunshine. You will be astonished at the number of beautiful long-stalked roses that can be cut in a rose-conservatory of this sort, not merely in spring but all summer through, and far into the autumn as well. Among the varieties that I would recommend for this purpose, Mme Butterfly, Ophelia, Grethel Greul, Talisman, Peace, Geheimrat Duisberg, Glory of Rome, Crimson Glory, and Mrs Pierre S. du Pont should be specially mentioned. It is this form of rose cultivation that is practised so successfully in the large rose forcing-houses in the suburbs of many of our towns and cities.

If you need something to climb up under your roof, or to cover a back wall you cannot do better than plant climbing hybrid teas—or Gloire de Dijon, Maréchal Niel and William Allen Richardson.

CHAPTER FIVE

Rose Propagation :
How it is carried out in Nurseries and
Market-Gardens

MOST CULTIVATED ROSES are the result of cross-breeding between purely wild roses (see next chapter) or between hybrids of wild forms. As the original true-to-seed parent has long been lost in the mists of time it is understandable that it is impossible to increase by sowing seed and expect the offspring to remain constant.

Recourse must be made to other means of propagation if one is to be able to multiply one's stock of this or that variety.

Increase from seed is only practicable in the case of pure wild roses.

The rose hips are collected in autumn, successively as the fruit ripens. They are then crushed, mixed with sand and stored in a flower-pot, box or frame, in a shady place until the following autumn. They must be kept damp and turned repeatedly; our object being, by exposure to air and water in the course of the summer, to make the rose seed so friable that the two halves, of which it is composed, will fall apart, releasing the kernel inside. When this is sown the following autumn, it will come in contact with the earth, and thus be given a chance of germinating. Nearly all wild-

74

rose seed must be treated in this way with the exception, perhaps, of that of *Rosa rugosa*, *Rosa multiflora* and *Rosa Wichuraiana* which may be sown the same autumn it is harvested.

The seed should be sown in clean, well-tilled earth in October, November or later, and is best sown in drills, and neither too deep nor too closely. If well cared for, good vigorous plants may be obtained in the course of a single summer. These can then be planted-out in readiness for budding.

The sowing and cultivation of wild roses is carried out on a large scale in special nurseries, and from here they are sold to nurseries that specialise in grafting and budding garden roses.

Garden roses of all categories may be increased in various ways and, as budding is the method most employed nowadays this will be described first.

'Budding' is done by taking an 'eye' or bud with a boat-shaped piece of bark behind, cut from a firm shoot of a garden-rose's past summer's growth, which is pushed under a T-shaped incision made in the bark of a wild rose and tied in with raffia.

It is easiest to buy the stocks, either a one-year seedling briar (*Rosa canina*) or seedlings and cuttings of *Rosa multiflora*, which, as mentioned before, are the most suitable and which will produce the most hardy plants for the purpose. They are obtainable with root necks varying from 3 to 5 mm and from 5 to 8 mm in thickness, of which the latter size is the most favourable for growth. They should be purchased in autumn, and their roots and head trimmed back; partly to facilitate planting, but also to ensure a more steady growth, and to improve the root system of the finished product. They are then 'heeled in' deep and closely packed in rows, and the soil is trodden firm. Next spring as early as possible, when the earth has become workable, they should be planted out, eight inches apart, in rows spaced some 2 feet 6 inches apart.

They must always be planted with the neck of the root above ground and in carrying out this operation, which is best effected with a large-size dibber, care should be taken that the roots are put in straight and that the plants are trodden firmly in place. The earth is then heaped up round the newly planted briars.*

In summer our roses must be kept free of weed and the soil kept loose manually, this latter operation being carried out at a nursery either by horse power or tractor. Late in July and during the whole of August is the best time for budding operations. This is the most important period in the year in a rose-nursery, and nurserymen fervently hope for warm dry weather at that time, for experience shows that warm, and even too-dry summer weather gives the best result.

* In large specialist nurseries planting is carried out more and more by tractor power, as it has been found necessary to rationalise the work in this field as in so many others. The drills in which the plants are placed being cut and the earth afterwards firmed down mechanically.

And now for the job itself. First of all we need a skilful operator (though skill, in this case, can only be attained through practice). It is not likely that budding will ever be carried out by machine. The operator must have a well-sharpened budding-knife provided with a handle tapering to a thin end for lifting the bark. The raffia for tying-in should be ready-cut in suitable lengths according to the thickness of the plants to be budded. A basket, in which to carry the budding-shoots, wrapped in moist canvas or grass, as they may be required as work proceeds along the rows. A pail of water, in which the supply of budding-shoots can be kept until needed, and preferably in the shade.

The heaped-up earth round the roses is now removed and the glossy clean necks of their roots stand revealed in all their pristine beauty.

The budding-shoots taken from the parent-rose should be chosen with care from healthy, vigorous plants; they should be shoots from which the bloom has but recently fallen, so that the buds in the axils of the leaves have not yet begun to put forth new shoots.

The plump lower buds on the shoot are the best and the ones best suited for our object. The leaves should be detached leaving a half-inch long leaf-stalk from which the two tiny leaflets on either side of the bud should be removed. The thorns should be carefully broken off, which it should be possible to do without the bark's breaking. If it does, the budding-shoot is not yet sufficiently ripened.

The operator now gets on with the job. Standing with legs firmly planted between the rows he takes a budding-shoot between the thumb and forefinger of his left hand (with the top end of the shoot towards his breast) and making a shallow incision, beginning about half an inch below a bud with a properly trimmed leaf-stalk, he passes his knife between bark and wood, going slightly deeper behind the bud; when this has been passed, he grasps the bud between knife and thumb and, with a careful jerk upwards, rips the bud from the shoot (which he sticks in his mouth). Then, holding the budding scion carefully between the thumb and forefinger of his left hand, he carefully removes the thin piece of wood behind the bud, taking extreme care that in doing so, he does not detach the germ of the bud. (N.B. If on holding to the light, the hollow containing the bud looks transparent, the germ of the bud has been removed, and another bud must be substituted, or failure will certainly follow.)

Bending down over the rose plant the operator looks under the branches for an even and smooth part of the neck and makes a horizontal incision just deep enough to sever the bark, and then from below a one inch long perpendicular slit up to it. Then, slightly twisting the blade, he separates the edges of the two sides of the T-shaped cut, so that, with the flat end of the handle, he can open them fully and push in the scion to the bottom of the opening in the bark. If the top end projects above the cross cut it must be cut off flush with it. He then proceeds to tie it in carefully and firmly so that the bud itself projects without being covered by the raffia.

As work proceeds along the rows the earth is heaped back, so that the budded neck and lower branches are completely covered as before. When things are being done on a large scale the work is shared by several workers, one for uncovering the roots, one for the actual budding, one for tying-in, and one for heaping the earth back again. A practised budder, when aided by his assistants, can easily work 100 roses an hour, and it is said that some operators can manage as many as 200! However that may be, an alert and practised worker will always achieve the better result.

In warm weather it will seldom take more than a fortnight for the bud to grow fast on to the wild root.

Incidentally I might mention that budding-shoots may be exchanged between different countries—usually the exchange of new varieties is effected in this way. Even consignments as far as to or from America have been despatched and used with a successful result.

It may be beneficial, if not actually necessary in September to remove the heaped-up earth round the budded rose-roots, to allow air and sunshine to ripen the buddings, but before November arrives they must be covered up again to protect them from winter frosts.

In latter years it has, however, become ever more customary not to earth up the plants immediately after budding, but to wait until the near approach of winter. The experts are still disputing about this point, and both methods are still being used—apparently with equal success. The early earthing-up method was originally introduced to protect the buddings from the red bud borer which ate its way in under the bud and the newly-formed callus, thus causing it to wither.

Next spring, early in April (in England February or March), the heaps are levelled down and the wild heads of the roses are cut off down to the transverse incision just above the budded scion. If everything has been done properly and the operation has been successful, a juicy red shoot will soon make its appearance. This should be pinched above the fourth leaf to encourage the development of side-shoots thus making for a thickly branched specimen. From early in July the young rose plants should begin to bloom and will usually continue to do so the entire summer through.

In addition to the *Rosa canina* mentioned above, other kinds of roses may also be used as under-stocks. *Rosa multiflora* seedlings, for instance, make excellent stocks for roses in flower-pots, and roses for forcing, but *Rosa canina* is the better stock for our climate. All the large-flowered garden-roses attain a far better colour and shape and probably also live longer than roses budded on any other stock, though *Rosa rubiginosa* seems to give much the same result as the dog-rose.

Increasing roses from cuttings was practised much more frequently in former days than is the case today. Especially the French nurseries in Orleans, at the end of last century and early in the present, raised almost all their monthly and tea roses from cuttings.

The best time to take rose cuttings is in July.

For this purpose a hot-bed with wind-proof lights is required. This should be sited with the sloping roof pointing northwards; the earth should be well mixed with peat fibre and sand, be well broken up, and topped off with a layer of washed sand with a little peat-dust mixed in. The cuttings should consist of half-ripened wood in three-leaved lengths and be cut just below and just above a leaf, the two lower leaves being removed entirely. The cutting is inserted for three-quarters of its length to the bottom of the upper layer of sand, and the earth trodden in firmly around it. A sub-soil watering is given immediately and from now on the cuttings must be well tended with sprayings and, on hot days be given more copious waterings. When the cuttings have started to grow and are firmly established, they must be gradually hardened by first lifting, then removing the lights at night, and by finally taking them off altogether. The plants must be covered up the following winter and may be planted out in the open next spring. The reason why the hot-bed light should

F

slope northwards is to reduce the danger of scorching. On specially sunny days it may be necessary to provide extra shade.

Another and third method of propagation is by grafting. The chief importance of this method is when a quick increase of novelties is desired, or when forced roses are to be increased on a large scale for planting out in a hot-house. This is done in winter in a closed frame with bottom heat. The budding-shoots should not have been exposed to frost. They must therefore be obtained from roses grown indoors, or from roses grown in pots and forced in such a way that the young shoots can be used. Increase by grafting is therefore only of interest to the rose specialist.

The cultivation and propagation of roses is thus one of the foremost activities of gardening. Many people are employed in this field. Considerable capital lies invested in hot-houses and boiler plant for forcing roses in winter. By unremitting effort to improve, and with ever-advancing techniques, many of our well-managed nurseries are now able to supply us with roses all the year round.

Raising new sorts of roses from seed (hybridising)

In this book, in which I have been trying to give my readers a few pointers about roses, this very important subject cannot well be left out.

As mentioned before, our garden roses are a mixed product of many and various kinds of roses. It is, therefore, not difficult to understand that the laws of heredity, which hold good only as regards sorts and species that come true to seed, cannot be applied with plants of such very mixed descent.

Experience however, has indicated certain ruling laws that may be accepted, such as the fact that the mother plants must be healthy and not susceptible to mildew or black spot; that the mother must be vigorous, stiff branched and floriferous. The father's genes, as experience shows, are of greater influence on form and colour. While, as for perfume—which should accompany every rose as an inseparable characteristic—it may come and go, indeed, often disappear altogether, even though one may cross two strongly perfumed parents, only to reappear in the third or fourth generation.

Cross-breeding

The modus operandi is as follows: The year before making the attempts the varieties one intends to use should be potted in fresh clean earth without manure of any kind. Strong growth is not beneficial for setting seed. The first year the potted roses should stand in a bed buried to the rim, and be tended with the requisite water. In the autumn they must be taken in to spend the winter in a cellar or conservatory and be kept dry till the middle of February. They are then pruned and given one or other kind of manure. Forcing must be done slowly if one is to ensure the best possible development.

In all fertilisation of flowering plants, when the

pollen contained in the anthers at the ends of the stamens is ripe the anthers open, so that the pollen may be transferred to the ripe stigma, where it takes hold and finds its way down through the pistil to the seed which adheres to the inside wall of the hip. The transference of pollen to pistil may be effected by the wind, through the medium of bees, or, as is the case with roses, of itself, i.e. by self-pollination. To prevent this happening to our roses the ones which are to serve as female parents must have the stamens removed. This should be done a few days before the flower buds open, by cutting or plucking away the petals so as to be able to get at the stamens, and remove them with a sharp knife, or a pair of scissors before the pollen ripens, thus preventing self-pollination.

It is also advisable that the thus ill-treated roses be protected from unwelcome guests, such as bees, flies and other insects, by covering them immediately after the operation with thin gauze or muslin bags. In a few days the flower will be ripe enough to receive the pollen from the variety of flower one intends to employ as the male parent and which should, of course, be flowering at the same time. When the female stigma is fully mature and is in the right condition for pollination it should be moist and clammy. With a camel-hair brush or a wad of cotton-wool we now take some of the pollen from the open male parent which has, of course, not been deprived of its stamens and convey it to the moist stigmas of the female parent, afterwards replacing the muslin bag as before.

The pollen will take hold and in a few days will find its way down to the seed—and pollination is complete.

A sunny afternoon or at least in the middle of the day is the best time to conduct the operation because the atmosphere is then usually dry, and the pollen in the most powdery and workable condition.

By no means all the flowers one pollinates can be expected to 'take'. Some will fall off, presumably because fertilisation was not possible between the two varieties chosen, or because the female parent was not in a condition to bear fruit. There are certain roses that are wholly or almost sterile, and their way of continuing to grow a flower instead of forming hips—usually a virtue in the garden—is a difficulty with these roses that is hard to deal with when pollination is the object in view. Too little or too much water may also be the cause.

It also happens quite often that the hip fruit is attacked by grey mould, dries up, withers and bears no fruit. This can, however, be remedied, if, about a week after the pollinating operation, we dip the hip in a cupful of a solution of one or other of the more generally used fungicides, e.g. Mido-Special-Merkuri, or Bordeaux mixture and hold the hip immersed in it for some time.

In all hybridising, i.e. raising of new sorts of

roses, the object in view is to produce something new and better than any of the sorts we already possess in such exceptional numbers that one would have thought it impossible to produce anything that really is an improvement. And yet the work done in latter years has proved that it is indeed still possible to do so. By crossing Ophelia with the yellow Souvenir de Claudius Pernet we got Talisman which was quite new both in form and colour. The deep-red, fragrant Crimson Glory is better than any of its predecessors. Poulsen's Yellow was something never seen before in its class as the first pure yellow Polyantha hybrid; and last but not least, the two wonderful roses, Peace and Ena Harkness.

But to return to our muttons! If the hips that have been set are to ripen, the plants must be kept under glass until summer is so far on the way that they may be moved out into the garden and the pots half buried in the earth. Watering must in no wise be neglected or exaggerated and new growth must be prevented by removal of any new sprouts that appear.

The cross-bred hips which should be labelled with the name of the male parent, will ripen some time in November or December. They should be plucked when they are red or reddish-yellow, put in a bag of clean sand or peat-dust, and the names of both male and female parent are written on the bag. The bag is now stored in a cool place; possibly in a refrigerator adjusted above freezing

point, until the close of December or early in
January when the seed should be sown.

The rose-hips, which may contain from one to
twenty or twenty-five seeds should now be opened
and the seed sown in flower-pots or boxes in fresh
soil mixed with some sand or peat-litter. They
should be covered over with half an inch of sandy
tilth (2 parts of sand to 1 of soil) well watered and
placed in a light cool green-house in a temperature
of about 7 to 10 centigrade. In the course of three
or four weeks the seeds will begin to sprout, and
gradually, when the small seedlings fully develop
their two first leaves, they are carefully removed
and planted in small flower-pots containing the
same soil proportions as that in which they were
sown. Our object now is to keep our tender seedlings healthy and vigorous. The temperature
should therefore be kept relatively cool and uni-
form. All draught and dessication must be carefully
avoided, otherwise mildew and green-fly may
easily despatch our tender small seedlings, which
should be able to put forth branches that are
strong enough to be budded in August or September.

Do not be led to imagine you will always find
something new and valuable among your seedlings, however well you may have considered the
combinations. The chances are very small. Often
only one in a thousand, and some years not even
one; in many cases the object in view must be
pursued through several generations.

As an instance of this it may be related that Pernet-Ducher, the well-known French rose cultivator, began his search for the pure yellow large-flowered perpetual by crossing, in 1885, the pure yellow but only once flowering Persian Yellow into the Antoine Ducher hybrid perpetual, and that he only succeeded in 1920 thirty-five years after. The result was released to the trade under the name of Souvenir de Claudius Pernet.

Unfortunately this delightful rose requires a warmer climate than that of Denmark if it is to develop its large, full, golden-yellow blooms.

Only when our seedlings reach the flowering stage the next summer can one have some idea of their value, and make one's first selection. In point of fact one should have one's seedlings under observation for three or four years before forming an opinion of their advantages or faults.

I have said enough, in this bare outline of the work of hybridisation, to indicate the trouble, experience, and patience involved; but it is a fascinating occupation and one that he who has seen a new rose reveal its entrancing beauty, will find hard to give up.

Rose novelties may also develop of themselves, the so-called sports (mutations). Ellen Poulsen, Ophelia and many others are instances of this. How they suddenly appear is not yet known; but occasionally an otherwise normal plant will suddenly grow a branch which in form, colour and growth differs from the normal appearance of the rose in question. A red or rosy coloured sort may sport to a lighter shade, even to quite white, or possibly to a deep red tone. A perpetual will sometimes grow a stem that develops without flowering the first year. It has, of itself, changed that one branch to a climber form. The buds in the axils of the leaves of these new-departure branches may be budded, in July or August, into a wild-briar stock, and the following year will, perhaps, prove to have retained their new characteristics—be constant—in fact a new variety. Mme Butterfly, for instance, from Ophelia, the dark-red Ellen Poulsen from Ellen Poulsen and the Climbing Testout from the old, well-known Mme Caroline Testout.

There was a time when all roses had to be large and full; that was the taste of the eighties, and lasted until well into the present century. Not that I wish in any way to decry the grace and beauty of the old-fashioned roses. On the contrary. But tastes may well differ.

It was the light, elegant, pointed rose-blooms that first gave rise to the wish for a change and opened the eyes of rose cultivators to a new world of beauty. Unfortunately, as it proved, the tea-roses were unable to satisfy the demands made upon them, their stalks were too feeble and flabby and the plants were not truly hardy. On the other hand it seemed as though the hybrid teas, that strong and healthy type of rose, were going to fulfil all the requirements needed for a rose; but a

long time was to pass, and only in the years sub-
sequent to the first world war was this development accomplished, and has possibly reached its
climax in roses like President Hoover, Talisman,
Elite, Comtesse Vandal, Spek's Yellow, Fashion,
Irene and many others. Many quite mediocre
types have been released as novelties and improve-
ments during the intermediate years, all or most of
them with a faint promise of something in the
right direction in form, and often with quite good
colouring, but which turned out so loosely built
and miserable that when the flowers opened they
were without form or bearing and often revealed
but dull faded colours.

Among them, however, a few exceptionally
charming, purely single roses were raised. In this
connection I am thinking of single hybrid teas
like Dainty Bess and Innocence, but it was only on
the appearance of clustering, single-flowered polyanthas that this form of rose became known and
was accepted as a real garden rose that one could
plant and enjoy in one's own garden.

The British and Americans were the last to
accept it. With them the real change of taste came
about only when in Scandinavia and Germany the
lightly-filled Polyanthas came to the fore several
years before that; while the French still prefer the
doubles. Else Poulsen is not a true single, it is
true, but Karen and Kirsten Poulsen and Betty
Prior have the shape of a perfectly formed single
bloom, which was, of course the original form of

all roses, and moreover it was soon discovered that their lasting qualities were just as good as those of any large-flowered variety and their wealth of bloom was ten times the quantity.

Now please don't run away with the idea that this noble pastime is only carried on as a hobby, for even if, round about the world, there are distinguished amateurs like C. Mallerin in France, Mr A. Norman in England and Mr O. Soenderhousen (Civil Engineer) in this country, the raising of new varieties has lately been developed by many nurserymen into a regular industry. The race to win the All American Rose Selection and through it, by letters patent in this country, to get hold of some not unwelcome dollars is getting ever keener. The case of Peace which won a fortune for its owner is infectious. Francis Meilland's nurseries at Cap d'Antibes which I saw in 1952 was an experience. Thirty thousand young seedlings in a single bed, all punctiliously labelled and duly registered, and then try to imagine the meticulous labour entailed in working one's way through all these to that one and only specimen that is to conquer a world, for that is what Peace, his protégé, after the last world war, actually did.

A Sunday I spent in the Jardin des Bagatelles, those wonderful rose-gardens tended and kept up by the Paris préfecture, where rose novelties from all over the world valiantly contest for that dearly coveted gold medal, and to which judges and experts of all nationalities make respectful pilgrimage, was a glorious and memorable experience. The judging, in the morning, of the two-year-old roses, planted five by five in tiny beds among the lawns was a fascinating battle of beauty, followed by lunch in the Eiffel Tower Restaurant. The contest is annual and the competition fierce; points are given for form, colour, freedom of blooming, perfume, healthy foliage and growth. In the afternoon the corps de ballet from the Opera was to have danced among the roses, but this had to be cancelled on account of rain. Instead we were generously invited to the Moulin Rouge and champagne, which was not less fascinating!

This then is a brief outline of a single rose workshop—and there are not a few equally large, or larger; and of the test the new roses have to go through before they can be recognised, and possibly later win a place in the sun, and, with luck, even win an American, a Dutch, a German or an Italian patent. Until recently these were the only countries with plant patent rights, though other countries (not including England) are now following suit. Thus by patenting his rose the lucky winner may gain a little encouragement for all the lengthy and expensive labour he has spent in raising the new variety.

What the future of roses is to be I cannot prophesy, but that new forms and types will develop is a foregone conclusion. There will always be a large assortment for the lover of roses to choose from. Possibly at some time in the future we shall develop a completely hardy garden rose, though even roses cannot very well grow up to the sky!

CHAPTER SIX

Modern Roses—Varieties - Colour - Group Planting and position in a Garden

A ROSE COLLECTION will always consist of the best of the new, the rather new and a few of the very old varieties which, in our climatic conditions, have proved themselves in possession of so many good qualities, as regards health, hardiness, colour, form and foliage, that they have been able to hold their own through the years in open market without being ousted by the ever rushing stream of later novelties. Moreover, there are always changes of taste, and continual stages of improvement. The period immediately after the last world war was in no wise behindhand in this respect, having given up many valuable new varieties, and made many a good step forward.

Even if the new varieties that appear from time to time do not always spell improvement, it must be admitted that rose varieties in general assuredly do improve as time goes on. And not merely in form, colour and fertility, but also their fragrance —that most precious quality—seems to have kept in step with the development. It would be wrong to suppose that most modern roses lack the quality of fragrance. On the contrary, I almost venture to assert that far and away the greater proportion of our modern, large-flowered garden roses are fully on a par, in this respect, with any of their much-lauded sisters in the days of our grandparents.

Only cluster-flowered roses (polyanthas) are not yet sufficiently developed to have fragrance as well as their many eminent qualities. It would seem difficult, somehow, to marry their extraordinary profusion of bloom to the typical old-fashioned fragrance of the teas and centifolias. Yet types like Ellen Poulsen and Anne-Mette Poulsen cannot be quite denied this virtue. We may surely take it for granted that, in the not too distant future, this drawback will be remedied.

In the meantime this type of rose has been greatly improved. The colours have become more brilliant; fragrance has been restored; and the roses that will be offered for sale in coming years will certainly possess this latter virtue in full measure.

Thus far I have written a good deal about the wild briar and the origins of the rose, so I think in the present chapter I ought to deal a little more with such garden roses, large-flowered polyanthas, climbers and certain specially fine, floriferous bedding roses as have not yet been mentioned save in my remarks about family relations and which, on account of their wealth of bloom and general make up, may well be included under the general title of Modern Garden Roses.

So here follows an assortment of these kinds of roses arranged in order of colour, beginning at one end with darkest red and going over gradually to crimson, rose-red and pink and on to pale-pink and white, then, rising again through white and pale-cream to pure yellow, orange-yellow, orange-pink and finally up to blood-orange and copper-red varieties.

Very possibly this arrangement of sorts according to colour, which has been made without the help of a colour-scale, is not by any means exact. But then, the colour of a rose is often a mixture of various shades of colour, and these colours may well vary from spring to autumn, as every rose-lover knows. I have therefore tried to arrange my list according to the most dominant colour of each at midsummer, and it is my hope that this tentative attempt may prove of help and assistance in guiding my readers' choice.

As you see, the list is made out in two sections, one for large-flowered roses, and one for those with blooms in clusters (polyanthas).

The first list comprises good, large-flowered garden roses belonging to the hybrid teas and Pernetiana types, without the fact being specially stated—except in the case of hybrid perpetuals—as these require special methods of pruning (see Pruning).

These lists do not even pretend to be complete, and I know that I shall be criticised for not having included more or various other varieties. My only defence is that, wherever possible, I have endeavoured to reduce the list to sizable proportions, and, often also, tastes differ.

It is also quite probable that in a few years this selection will have to be revised again in order to insert newer and better sorts in place of some of those included above.

Those who care to compare the first with the second edition of this 'book about roses' will notice quite a change in the selections made, as indeed in my conception of what is good. This is due not merely to the arrival of many new-comers after the end of the last world war, but also to the fact that many of those raised by nurserymen and amateurs all over the world prior to and during the war now, on being tried out in our gardens, prove that peaceful occupations like rose-growing may go on and even thrive prodigiously though a whole world be on fire. More, during that period an advance was made that far surpasses that of preceding years.

The best large-flowered garden roses

As to the captional descriptions of the various varieties selected I shall endeavour to make them as brief as possible.

ABBREVIATIONS

*Specially suitable for planting in large groups:

VF	Very fragrant.	VT	Very tall.
MF	Medium fragrance.	T	Tall.
WS	Weak scent.	M	Medium.
	D	Dwarf.	

The roses in the following selection not marked with a * should not be considered less suitable for grouping on that account.

G

A 'grouping' rose can sometimes only be planted in that way and in no other, while of nearly all other garden roses it may be said that they may be planted either singly or in groups. But whether in a rose-bed, in a vase or on view at a flower show almost all are entrancingly beautiful. I hope my readers will understand that I am a gardener and not a writer, and will therefore try to imagine what (if I could) I should like to say. A dog must have a name, and any attempt at painting with mere words is like trying to describe one's loved one to a friend. It is simply impossible. The very poverty of words is an unsurmountable obstacle. He cannot borrow your eyes, or possibly conjure up the picture as you see it.

A rose at its best should be seen early on a June morning with the dew still glistening on its leaves and blossoms. Or just before sunset, when its colours seem to gleam with a warmer and somehow more ethereal radiance than at any other time.

The following colour-scheme rings the changes from dark ruby red through pink, white and yellow, to orange.

Fragrance Height

COUNTESS DANNESKIOLD-SAMSOE. Reddish-black *VF* *T* to deep red, conical buds, semi-double, delightful.

CHARLES MALLERIN. A glorious play of colour *MF M* from warm crimson to dark red, large tightly-filled flowers. A lover of sunshine and warm summers.

Fragrance Height

*CRIMSON GLORY. Reddish-black to dark red. *VF T* Shapely, pointed blooms. Very prolific and floriferous.

*ETOILE DE HOLLANDE. Clear dark-red, large, *VF D* shapely buds and blooms. One of our best and most hardy garden-roses.

NEW YORKER. A coming rose. The blooms are *MF M* double and well formed. They open slowly and keep their brilliant dark-red colour to the last. The growth is vigorous, free-flowering and healthy. An excellent rose for the garden, for decoration or for forcing.

BRILLIANT (Schloessers Brillant). The large, *WS T* round, conical buds develop into unusually large, completely double, brilliant-red blooms. Their colour is fast in the sun, and does not turn blue as the flowers fade. The growth is erect and healthy.

*ENA HARKNESS. A recent English variety of *MF M* intrinsic worth. The colour is flaming red, the shape ideally conical. Healthy and prolific and therefore flowers freely. This is an ideal rose, and one we have long been hoping for. It has no defects or blemishes, and no unfortunate tinges of black or blue. Definitely a rose that will be planted more and more often to the pleasure of all and the pain of none.

*POINSETTIA. Buds and blooms pointed and *WS M* shapely. Colour fiery red. Growth prolific and healthy and therefore very floriferous.

*GENERAL MACARTHUR. Flattish-double, crim- *VF T* son, very prolific, very free-flowering and hardy.

Fragrance Height

RUBAIYAT. Brilliant red with somewhat paler *MF M*
reverse. Good upright growth and wealth of
foliage.

HUGH DICKSON (hybrid perpetual). Dark-red. *VF VT*
Large tightly packed flowers, pointed buds.
Very vigorous and hardy.

ULRICH BRUNNER (hybrid perpetual). Cherry- *VF T*
red, round, inward-bent, old-fashioned shape.
Suitable for hedges or large groupings.

*GRANDE DUCHESSE CHARLOTTE. Orange to *MF T*
tomato-red. The blooms are large, elongated,
semi-double. Healthy growth, prolific and free-
flowering. Characteristic, very healthy.

*OPERA. Egg-shaped buds, charmingly double *VF M*
and when fully open of great beauty. The
colour scheme is something between scarlet and
copper-red, a colour not often seen in roses. A
lovely flower for the garden or cutting.

*TALLY-HO. Buds round, developing into large, *VF M*
well-shaped, double blooms. The flowers are
crimson in centre with a cardinal-red reverse, a
charming colour contrast. The plant is prolific
and healthy. Constant bloomer and floriferous.

MISSION BELLS. A rose without fault or blemish. *MF M*
The colour varies between light salmon-pink
and lobster-red. Buds and blooms an ideal
shape and the plant is healthy and prolific.

*CHARLOTTE ARMSTRONG. Rose-red. One of the *VF M*
best of the new-comers of recent years. Shape,
colour, flowers, growth and fragrance, all are
present and in rich measure.

Fragrance Height

*KATHERINE T. MARSHALL. Another recent rose *MM*   *F* in which growth, foliage and floriferousness are all good. The shape and colour of the blooms is excellent. In this case a warm rose-pink.

DAME EDITH HELEN. Warm pink, closely packed *VF*   *T* blooms. Stiff, erect growth. Good for decoration and when planted in groups.

MRS JOHN LAING (hybrid perpetual). Light pink, *VF VT* large, buxom, well built.

*MRS HENRY BOWLES. Pink, shot with salmon- *MF*   *D* pink shadings, good firm growth, well-built blooms and buds.

MADAME GABRIEL LUIZET (hybrid perpetual). *VF VT* Silky pink, old-fashioned, round, closely packed blooms.

THE DOCTOR. Brilliant, unblemished pink, large *MF*   *D* loosely-built blossoms. Needs warm, sheltered situation.

*MADAME CAROLINE TESTOUT. One of the good *WS*   *T* old hybrid teas. Is included here for the sake of its prolific, healthy growth, its profusion of blooms and great hardiness. The colour is silky pink.

*EDITH NELLIE PERKINS. Light salmon-pink *MF M* with closely packed pointed blooms and buds. Healthy, prolific and extremely hardy.

*PICTURE. Light pink. Has the well-turned, *MF*   *D* pointed bud and bloom of the perfect rose. It is also, at all times, the clean, neat and tidy, grouping rose.

Fragrance Height

EDEN ROSE. A Peace seedling, and as such, has MF T
inherited many of its good qualities, such as:
health, fresh green foliage, erect vigorous
growth and, last but not least, large and delightfully perfect blooms. The colour is a clear
cherry-red with a faint tinge of yellow in the
centre. It is easy to grow, is very durable, and
the blooms are excellent for decoration.

ROYALIST. Tyrian rose-pink, exceptionally MF M
vigorous, cedar-green foliage.

*VERSCHUREN'S PINK. Unblemished pink; large- MF M
flowered; buds and blooms a well-turned, peg-
top shape and semi-double. Prolific, healthy,
floriferous and hardy.

MRS HENRY MORSE. Light pink tinged with pale WS M
yellow; exceptionally lovely, well-shaped
blooms and buds. Rather susceptible to mildew
in autumn.

DAINTY BESS. Light pink, single blooming, WS T
quite enchanting.

*MADAME BUTTERFLY. Light pink with yellow MF D
shadings. Excellent for forcing and decoration.
Exceptionally well-shaped blooms.

*OPHELIA. Salmon-flesh shaded with yellow, MF D
well-known as good for forcing and decoration,
and, like all Ophelia roses, an excellent all-
round garden rose.

*MICHÈLE MEILLAND. The blooms are large, VF M
double and exceptionally durable. The colour
is a pure, unchanging pink. The plant is prolific, healthy and floriferous. A lovely rose for
garden and decoration.

Fragrance Height

FRAU KARL DRUSCHKI (hybrid perpetual). Well-　— *VT*
known, snow-white, shapely rose, but not very
suitable for planting among other roses.

VIRGO. In this rose we have, maybe, found the　*MF M*
quite ideal snow-white rose. A shapely form,
and lovely even as it withers. Healthy and
prolific.

*BLANCHE MALLERIN. Chaste, alabaster-white　*VF M*
and of extraordinary beauty. The plant is
healthy and prolific and quite exceptionally
floriferous.

INNOCENCE. Large, open, pure-white with only　— *D*
two rows of petals. The shape of the lovely
flowers, the yellow stamens and the healthy,
vigorous growth make it a garden rose of exceptionally high standard.

*LUNA. Lightish-yellow to yellowish-white.　*VF M*
Large shapely flowers and buxom buds. Considered by many to be the best in its class.

*ROSLYN. Light-yellow with wavy petals and　*WS M*
shapely blooms of characteristic form.

*GEHEIMRAT DUISBERG. Yellow, very free-　*MF D*
flowering; good, well-formed, pointed flowers
and buds, very similar to Ophelia varieties, and
may be used for the same purposes.

ROSELANDIA. Dull-yellow. Good autumn　*MF M*
bloomer. Shapely, pointed blooms and buds.

*ECLIPSE. Golden-yellow with slender semi-　*VF D*
double buds, often as much as $2\frac{1}{2}$ in. long, en-
closed in grass-green sepals. This variety is
prolific, floriferous and hardy and is excellent
for the garden and for decoration.

Fragrance Height

*PEACE. A peerless, large double, durable, dis-   *MF D*
tinctive bloom. The colour, on opening, is
yellow. Later on the edges of the petals turn a
lovely pinkish-white and then change entirely
as the flower matures. It does not wither, but
dies in beauty. The plant and foliage are
healthy, robust and extremely hardy. Peace
has been the most talked of rose since the war,
and, having bewitched a world of rose-lovers,
is, perhaps, the most planted of all varieties in
all countries. Its virtues are legion and universal. Of faults it has none. The foliage is so
full-bodied and glossy that even without
flowers the plant is delightfully decorative. But
there are *always* flowers, large as Chinese
peonies and equally exquisite whether in bud
or in bloom. They are carried on powerful,
vigorous stalks and last extraordinarily long.
The colour in the bud stage is yellow striped
with red. On opening fully, the blooms are
pure yellow. This quickly changes, in the
outer petals, to a pink and rosy tone. The
blossoms do not fade or wither, but discard their
beauty while it is still there, and yet they last
longer than do the blooms of most of their sisters.

*MRS PIERRE S. DU PONT. Deep golden-yellow *MF M*
with shapely pointed buds and blooms. This
is one of the best roses for grouping. It is very
floriferous and presents a well-balanced, prolific growth.

*SPEK'S YELLOW. Medium-sized, double blooms *MF M*
of perfect shape, often growing in clusters. The
growth is prolific and flowering is continuous.
The colour is a durable, brilliant, sunny yellow.
A delightful garden and cut rose. Is also one
of the best for forcing.

Fragrance Height

SUTTER'S GOLD. From America. A lovely, *VF VT* healthy and wide-awake sort. The buds are longish and burst to reveal large, charmingly-coloured, golden-yellow blooms, which are often set singly on singularly long stalks.

MARCELLE GRET. The large, chaste, orange- *MF VT* yellow blooms of this variety keep their colour even while fading. The growth is vigorous and erect, and the foliage glossy-green and disease-proof.

FOLIES BERGÈRE. The large, egg-shaped buds *VF D* open to reveal closely packed, double, charm-ingly perfumed blossoms. The colour is yellow with copper-red shadings. The plant is prolific and very floriferous.

SOUVENIR DE JACQUES VERSCHUREN. A glorious *VF M* light-orange, in which growth and flowering are profuse, prolific and healthy.

*CYNTHIA BROOKE (McGredy, 1942). A curi- *VF M* ously characteristic, healthy grouper, carrying large, double, leather-yellow blooms standing stiffly on rigid stalks. Very durable and de-corative.

MEVROUW G. A. VAN ROSSEM. Dark, apricot- *VF M* yellow and orange, with large portly flowers giving it a strange beauty.

*TALISMAN. Copper-yellow shot with scarlet *MF T* and orange, a glorious combination of colours. Shape, growth, and foliage all make this rose one of the best for every purpose.

Fragrance Height

*MCGREDY'S SUNSET. As magnificent as a sum- *VF* *T*
mer sunset. The petals are butter-yellow,
tinged with orange outside and scarlet inside.
The blooms which have the ideal shape stand
out nobly on this prolific healthy plant.

*FLAMING SUNSET. Is a sport of the above with *VF* *T*
an even stronger play of colours.

*PRESIDENT HERBERT HOOVER. Many coloured; *VF* *T*
the large perfectly formed flowers with their
many shades of scarlet, yellow, and cherry-red,
are carried on long rigid stalks thus making it
specially suitable for cutting and a good bedder.

TEXAS CENTENNIAL. A darker sport of the above *VF* *T*
but with more orange and reddish purple.

*CONDESA DE SÁSTAGO (Dot, 1933). The bud is *VF* *M*
chrome-yellow appearing to promise a yellow
bloom. The yellow is kept concealed, but when
the blooms are fully open, exposing the rasp-
berry-red inner sides of the petals, the yellow
is not frogotten. The growth is erect, vigorous
and healthy.

*BETTY UPRICHARD. Crimson to salmon-flesh *MF* *T*
on an orange background. A really good,
healthy and willing grower whose flowers keep
their form and colour long after they have been
cut. With this rose in your garden you can
always depend on a good summer display.

R.M.S. 'QUEEN MARY' (Mev. H. A. Verschuren). *WS* *M*
Salmon-pink to orange, a rose of fascinating
form and colour. The blooms are carried on
long, rigid stalks.

Fragrance Height

*LUIS DE BRINAS. The blooms are of a vivacious *WF* *T*
orange-pink colour and while fading are still
large and delightful. The plant is healthy and
conspicuously floriferous and hardy.

*MCGREDY'S SALMON. Tall, well formed bush *MF* *T*
with pointed buds and double blooms. The
foliage is dark and healthy. Growth vigorous.

MARGARET MCGREDY. Orange-tinged scarlet, the *WS* *T*
fully double blooms when quite open turn
crimson-pink. The growth is healthy and
vigorous assuring us of a wealth of flower from
July to late autumn.

HECTOR DEANE. Pointed buds, double blooms, *VF* *M*
shapely form. Colour a mixture of orange,
cochineal and salmon-pink, long stalked and
prolific. The foliage glittering green. Healthy.

COMTESSE VANDAL. Copper and salmon-pink. *WS* *M*
A delightful rose from the first colouring of the
prettily turned, pointed buds till the last petals
fall.

*GRETEL GREUL. Dark sport of Ophelia. A de- *MF* *D*
lightful rose in the garden, house or as a cut
flower. The colour is orange-red and pink.
No one will regret the presence in his garden
of this glorious rose.

ELITE. An extremely healthy, vigorous plant *WS* *M*
which always carries its delightful flowers singly
on long rigid stalks freely above the foliage.
The colour, which remains unchanged till the
flowers fall, is salmon-pink with shades of
orange.

The small-flowered garden roses—The 'clustering' or polyantha roses, or also, as Americans call them, the floribunda roses.

In its original form, the pure polyantha rose is now but little used, whereas the more recent polyantha-hybrids, called by many (also abroad) the 'Poulsen type', are planted so much the more. They are all typical group or bedding roses and as such have gained an extraordinarily widespread distribution. This is especially the case under large-scale conditions where, on account of their wealth of bloom and great hardiness, they have not merely superseded the large-flowered garden roses but have also been used and are still being used to replace former annual summer flowers, thus entailing a welcome reduction in the annual budget. They are also eminently suitable for the perennial border where, by suitable planting together with the perennials that form their background, they can achieve far better colour effects than when standing alone.

A third typical characteristic of the polyantha-hybrids is the fact that the petals of the bloom are usually of such a consistency and durability that both in the flower-bed, and as cut flowers in a vase, they last considerably longer than we are accustomed to with hybrid teas. This peculiarity, as far as certain sorts are concerned, might be thought a fault that has to be remedied by incessantly removing withered blooms from their stalks. There are those who consider it a virtue, however, for, as they say, it is far less trouble to pick off the withered blooms than it is to pick them up.

They may be used as flowering hedges and thus used, are often of excellent effect. In the following list the varieties best suited for use in this way will be marked with an (*H*) after the name. The letters used for fragrance and height will be the same as those used for the large-flowered varieties.

Fragrance Height

POULSEN'S CRIMSON. Polyantha-hybrid, semi-double, rather big flowers gathered in clusters as capacious bouquets. The colour is a conspicuously brilliant dark-red crimson, that gleams and glows in the sunlight. The plant is healthy and is one of the most floriferous of its kind. *MF D*

ALAIN. Polyantha-hybrid. The blooms, which are usually gathered in large clusters, are double crimson-red, and very durable. As the plant flowers continuously until late harvest it is an excellent garden-rose. It is also healthy and hardy. *MF T*

FRENSHAM (*H*). Polyantha hybrid. The shapely dark red blooms are gathered in large, or somewhat smaller clusters, which flower continuously all summer and till late harvest. The foliage is fresh and healthy and it is possibly the best of recent red roses suitable for hedges, large beddings and in the front row of bush plantings. *— VT*

Fragrance Height

KARL WEINHAUSEN. Polyantha-hybrid. The — VT
blooms are durable, semi-double, collected in
clusters and remain unaltered while blooming.
The colour is clear dark-red and never turns
black or bluish. This healthy towering plant
may be planted as a hedger, a bushy bedder or
may stand alone. It will hold its own wherever
it is.

FANAL. Polyantha-hybrid. The large almost — T
completely single blooms are put forth in a
continuous profusion of flower all summer
through. The colour is bright red and is very
durable. A healthy, prolific sort especially
suitable for beds and large groupings.

ANNE-METTE POULSEN. Polyantha-hybrid. The MF M
large, semi-double, fiery red blooms, the wavy
petals, yellow stamens and large clusters of
blooms all go to make a plant of quite exceptional beauty.

COMMONWEALTH (Herzblut). Polyantha-hybrid. — M
This radiantly bright, blood-red, large-flowered
semi-double variety will certainly be much in
demand in coming summers.

MARGO KOSTER FULGENS. A pure red sport of — D
Margo Koster (the Parisian rose), an excellent,
not too tall, garden rose that is good for forcing.

ATOMBOMBE. Novelty. Polyantha-hybrid. — T
Large double blooms set in very large clusters.
The colour is brilliant scarlet without other
shadings. The blooms last well. The foliage is
healthy and the form well-built-up and shapely.

Fragrance Height

GERTRUD WESTPHAL. A German novelty. Poly- — D
antha-hybrid, semi-double blooms growing in
pretty close-set clusters. The colour, a scarlet
red, glows with such radiance that one's eyes
are caught and held by it. The plant is of creeping growth, is thickly branched and covered
with healthy green foliage.

COCORICO. A polyantha rose of Karen Poulsen — *VT*
type, but taller, and of an intensive tile-red
colour. The wealth of large, single, strongly-
coloured blooms, and its healthy, prolific
growth, will certainly secure this rose a place
in many a garden of the future.

KAREN POULSEN. Brilliant red. The colour is — *T*
extremely durable even in burning sunlight.
The single blooms are set in large clusters and
flowering is continuous.

INDEPENDENCE (Kordes Sondermeldung). A *MF T*
polyantha-hybrid with the floral character of a
tea-hybrid. The large, well-formed blooms are
set singly, either several together or in large
clusters. The plant is healthy and hardy,
blooms continuously, and its colouring looks
like velvet in the sun. Excellent in the garden,
for decoration or for forcing. Will certainly be
in widespread cultivation in coming years.

KIRSTEN POULSEN (*H*). Polyantha-hybrid. A — *VT*
well-known, single, older variety that is now
planted mostly in hedges or in large groupings.
It is unusually hardy and healthy. Light
cherry-red.

Fragrance Height

NINA POULSEN. Unblemished, dark cherry-red. —   T
Grows something like Rødhætte (Little Red
Riding-Hood) but is taller and grows more
freely. Hardy and healthy.

ELLEN POULSEN. Dark Red. A darker sport of   MF   D
the well-known Ellen Poulsen and is of similar
growth and characteristics.

TIVOLI. Also a new-comer that will certainly   MF   T
please garden-lovers present and future. This
variety was awarded the Award of Merit in
London in 1953 and in Paris in 1953, where it
gained the highest points of any hybrid polyantha shown. The blooms are large, semi-
double and cherry-red on a yellow ground.
Free growing, free flowering and exceptionally
healthy. Fresh green foliage.

HEIDEKIND. Hybrid polyantha. Quite large,   MF   D
double, coral-pink blooms. Said to be a hybrid
of *Rosa rugosa* and is therefore very hardy. An
excellent garden rose in every way.

BARONESS MANON. Hybrid polyantha. Yet   MF   T
another large-flowered cluster rose with the
character of a hybrid tea, and may thus well
be planted among these. The growth is robust
and prolific. The strong shoots are covered
with large, powerful thorns. The foliage is
attractive and the whole plant floriferous and
pleasing. It sometimes continues to flower till
late into October or even till early November.
The blooms are tightly-packed double, and
their colour light-crimson.

POULSEN'S BEDDER (*H*). Hybrid polyantha. One   MF   T
of the very best tall polyanthas. Healthy,
hardy and prolific. Blooms continuously from

Fragrance Height

July to late November, never in exceptionally
large clusters, but is always in flower, and lasts
beautifully in vases. The colour is a lovely pink
with a slightly yellowish tone. Semi-double and
of medium size.

ELLEN POULSEN. Light cherry-pink. The   *MF D*
shapely double blooms are gathered in large
clusters. The leaves are a fresh, glossy green.
It quickly starts a second display, and is vigorous and healthy.

CROWN PRINCESS INGRID. Hybrid polyantha. A   — *D*
dark pink, large-flowered, almost single rose of
Else Poulsen type, but contrary to the latter is
immune against mildew.

ORANGE TRIUMPH. A polyantha that is possibly   — *T*
one of the most planted cluster rose. The
blooms are double and set in very large clusters.
The colour is a clear, orange-scarlet. It is a
vigorous grower and flowers continuously till
late autumn. Both health and longevity faultless.

MÄRCHENLAND (*H*). German new-comer. The   — *VT*
blooms are unusually large in size and bulk.
The colour is light-pink with a strong tinge of
salmon-flesh. The growth is vigorous and tall.
Its willingness to flower is quite exceptional.

ELSE POULSEN. Hybrid polyantha, of a clear,   — *T*
unblemished pink which is, however, somewhat
darker in the bud stage. The semi-double,
shapely flowers are set in large flattish umbels,
and last extremely well. It is thus an excellent
rose for decoration. The growth is erect and
vigorous, but after the first display the plant is
often attacked by mildew. Very careful tending
is advisable.

H

Fragrance Height

ELSE POULSEN. Improved. Hybrid polyantha. —   *D*
A seedling of the above and is so similar in
blooms, colour, shape and growth that it is
rightly entitled to bear the name. It is, however, slightly less prolific and the flower clusters
are somewhat smaller, but these are the only
differences. Should be planted in somewhat
closer groupings (mildew-proof).

MEVROUW NATHALIE NYPELS. Hybrid polyantha. —   *D*
Light pink with medium-full blooms. A charming little rose, suitable for vase or for table
decoration. A good bloomer also in autumn.

POULSEN'S PINK. Hybrid polyantha. Light pink *MF   T*
with tinge of yellow spreading from centre.
Flowers long and profusely. The foliage is
fresh-looking and the growth prolific. It is one
of the few roses of which only good can be said.

MRS INGE POULSEN. Hybrid polyantha. A *F   D*
novelty. Light-pink on a yellow base tinged
with salmon-pink. The blooms are double and
gathered in large clusters. A prolific and very
vigorous rose.

BETTY PRIOR (*H*). Belongs to that vigorous type —   *VT*
that can be planted as a hedge between one's
rose-bushes or may be allowed to grow and
develop either as a solitary bush or be planted
in threes, merely trimming it back slightly here
and there. In this way a completely constant-
flowering, prolific park-rose may be developed.
It is single and the colouring varies between
light and dark pink.

MRS JULIE POULSEN. Hybrid polyantha. This is —   *T*
a very characteristic variety. It is an almost

single, large-flowering, charmingly tender pink, shot with tinges of yellow. Carries a wealth of flower in large, loosely-set clusters. The foliage is reddish and dainty. Both in vases and in the garden it is highly decorative.

RØDOVREROSEN (Poulsen's Fairy) (*H*). Is of much the same type as Betty Prior. The colour and shape of the flowers is, however, much finer, reminding one of Dainty Bess with the latter's charming stamens and flesh-coloured pink blooms. It is highly prolific, healthy and enormously floriferous. — *T*

GRÜSS AN AACHEN PINK. Old-fashioned, large-flowered, clustering rose that has always been listed among the polyanthas, though, in fact, its foliage, growth and flowers more resemble the hybrid teas, to which category it very possibly belongs. It blooms prodigiously and throughout a very long period. *MF D*

GRÜSS AN AACHEN. Pink. This was the original variety which seems to hover between white and faint pink, while the above sways between pink and rose-red. It is thus a sport. The blooms are large, tightly packed and set in flat umbels. The displays, which come in waves, are prodigious. It is therefore a much planted variety. *MF D*

IRENE (Irene of Denmark). A Danish newcomer; a hybrid polyantha. It is a chalk-white, cluster rose, the blooms of which are full and formed almost like a gardenia. It flowers long and prodigiously. The foliage is light-green, with a delightfully fresh and glossy appearance. The branches are thornless. A very charming little variety. *MF D*

Fragrance Height

MARGO KOSTER WHITE. Another sport of the — T original 'Parisian Rose', this time a white. Occasionally—as is often the case with sports— the characteristics of the old Mother-plant strike through, and some of the blooms reveal an orange-red, red or pinkish striping.

DANISH GOLD. Hybrid polyantha. Clear canary- *MF* T yellow. The blooms, which become slightly paler as they fade, are of an exceptionally shapely form, both as buds and when fully open, when the two rows of petals form a delightful bowl round the pistils and stamens. The plant is prolific, healthy and floriferous, the branches being light-green, with few but serviceable red thorns.

POULSEN'S YELLOW. The first pure golden- *VF M* yellow polyantha. The buds, before breaking, are usually something between brilliant red to copper-red. The growth is graceful, slightly overhanging and the blooming prodigious. A plant in which foliage, colour of the branches and flowers form a delightful, harmonious whole.

COLUMBINE. Another new-comer. So new, *VF M* indeed, that it will not be on the market before 1955 or 1956, but, being so pleased with it myself, I cannot refrain from including it in advance, so to speak. It is, in a way, a Peace in miniature, but is, in reality a cross between Danish Gold and Frensham, and is therefore prodigiously floriferous and healthy. And then, what delightful fragrance! The shape of the flowers, the wonderful perfume and its growth are all they should be, if a rose is to be considered really good.

Fragrance Height

POULSEN'S SUPREME (Kelleris Rose) (*H*). A —   *T*
vigorous, healthy, floriferous plant with a constant wealth of orange-pink to yellow-pink, semi-
double blooms carried on long, erect stems. On
account of its great durability it is excellent for
indoor decoration, and from the bud stage to
the fully open flower it is extremely beautiful.

SUN DANCE. Is a new rose that was awarded a —   *T*
Gold Medal in London at the Summer Show
of 1954. It is a rose of Else Poulsen type.
While in bud it is an exquisite creamy yellow,
then, as it opens, it quickly changes to orange-
pink and finally to pure pink. The flowers are
extremely durable, both on the plant and when
cut. It is therefore eminently suitable for
indoor decoration. The foliage and branches
are light green, the thorns bright red and the
whole plant gives a delightful impression of
health and cleanliness.

MASQUERADE. Hybrid polyantha. An American —   *T*
novelty of quite astonishing colour effect. The
blooms which are set in large clusters are semi-
double and very durable. The buds are bright
red, the blooms when half open are pure
golden-yellow, only to change, in the fully open
blossom, back to red again; a colour contrast of
quite unusual effect, especially when many are
planted together.

MARGO KOSTER. Orange pink to pink, with the —   *D*
petals curling inwards. Especially suitable for
bouquets and indoor decoration. Among flor-
ists and market-gardeners this rose is known as
the 'Parisian Rose'.

Fragrance Height

FASHION. Another American hybrid-polyantha *VF M*
novelty. The blooms are a clear coral-pink, a
most delightful kind of colour because it seems
both chaste and utterly charming. And when
to this we add the shapely grace of its buds and
blooms it is not difficult to understand why, in
so few years, it has become so famous and is so
widely distributed.

If, in the case of the hybrid teas, as previously
mentioned, there has been such a striking and
revolutionary advance, this advance has been, if
possible, even greater in the case of the polyanthas.

The original small-flowered sorts like Mrs Cut-
bush and the Orleans Rose, etc., are hardly ever
grown nowadays, and rightly so; but many of the
early sorts, like Rødhætte (Little Red Riding
Hood) and others that we were all so enthusiastic
about twenty or twenty-five years ago should perhaps now be replaced in gardens and parks by
more recent and even better varieties. It is because
they are so healthy, hardy and vividly alive that
the old sorts are still allowed to carry on. Yet the
colours and shapely blooms of more recent varieties
are indubitably better; and then, they are in no
wise less healthy or less alive than were their
predecessors.

We shall be returning to this subject later, when
I shall try to suggest a few of the many and varied
possibilities there are for using these later sorts
which have so completely altered this type of rose,

bringing it, in many cases, ever nearer to the hybrid tea group.

It would seem more than likely that things will go in much the same way as they did with the Pernetiana roses which were originally listed separately as an individual group, but which, on being worked into the existing hybrid teas, were finally accepted under the common denomination.

There would seem to be every sign in sun and moon that things will turn out in the same way with the hybrid polyanthas. The individual differences are gradually becoming ever less and less distinct; the hybrid teas, through continual cross-breeding with them pass on ever more and more of their special characteristics: larger flowers, greater fragrance, a richer play of colour and larger and more robust leaves, make the difference ever less conspicuous. If only the new roses can keep intact the virile vigour and floriferousness of the polyanthas they will have an assured future—especially for growing under less favourable conditions. For the polyanthas are usually able to stand up to more cold and heat than do any of the hybrid teas.

Perhaps the American name for this type of rose, *Floribunda*, is a good choice. It has been adopted in England also. Very few of the newer varieties are in fact hybrid polyanthas.

CHAPTER SEVEN

Ramblers and Climbers

Notes on the life of the Roses in our Gardens, on their individual dispositions and various peculiarities

FOR THE MAN WHO TENDS HIS ROSES HIMSELF, and doesn't let things rest on a set of fixed rules—or prayers—there are many chances of unalloyed pleasure in a garden, and he will quickly discover that roses have their own individual tastes and dispositions. One thing, however, is common to them all: they prefer to stretch themselves in sunshine and light, and to spread themselves over other plants; over a lavender-bush, for instance, or anything growing within reach. And why not? By all means let them do so!

It may be necessary to move a perennial or two, a mossy alpine, or indeed other roses, and to swivel the lawn-mower in a graceful curve round this or that extra virile specimen. But just let it stand intact—or even assist it if you can! Don't be too ruthless with that pruning-knife or secateur of yours, and, whatever you do, don't cut your roses back before they have finished flowering, and even then not too severely.

If you've time and inclination, give them a weekly teaspoonful of nitrogen manure diluted in one of your small watering-cans, and a tablespoonful of nitrate of calcium [Ca $(NO_3)_2$] or sulphate of ammonia [$(NH_4)_2SO_4$] in your big one and let it have a dose every week. It will work wonders! You will be surprised at the amount of sickness and misery that will disappear—seemingly of itself —after this treatment. If it is a question of one of the large-flowered varieties being pruned back to a single flower on each stalk, there will be more surprise at the size the remaining flowers will attain, their greatly enhanced colour, and the speed with which the blooms replace themselves. Of course, your rose-beds should have the usual spring dressing of powdered hoof and horn or mixed manure, for it is only when your roses are well established that it is wise to play tricks with them. The same method may be tried with climbers and many other plant inhabitants of the garden. If one tends one's plants properly, there is, for instance, almost no limit to the height and appearance of a larkspur, or to how luxuriant and prolific a phlox may become.

It may also happen that a rambler will spread itself outside its intended domain. If there is any likelihood of this, by all means let it do so, nay, assist it rather, give it useful supports, tie it up securely, and be as lenient as possible with your pruning knife. A single Dr W. van Fleet may cover a whole summer-house or pergola, may creep up to and over a roof, up into a tree, and over any support it may find handy. Also here, the little weekly dose will work wonders. A *Rosa*

Hugonis, a Maiden's Blush, a Celestial or whatever these glorious park roses may happen to be called, all will appreciate and respond to this individual attention, not to mention all the hybrid polyanthas which in themselves are ever so willing and anxious to grow, and so exuberantly prolific!

Almost any garden, properly tended, will entirely change in character, for the rose varieties now at our disposal have the ability, and given a reasonable chance, will not fail to provide flowers, fertility and fragrance. I still remember Mr Jens K. Joergensen, the Royal Danish Horticultural Society's masterly gardener. A trip with him round his beloved gardens was always a noteworthy experience, enlivened as it usually was by his pithy remarks: 'Why coddle a plant—a rose, for instance—that does not thrive? Root it out, man, and let the more willing workers have a chance.' It is the general aspect of luxuriance, the prolific abundance of bloom, and the strikingly healthy foliage that gives this tiny parklet its very special character, and, even though one may have one's own preferences, there are no plants that are downright ugly. I shall refrain, in this connection, from mentioning sorts and kinds of roses that have already been described elsewhere in this book, where precise information is given as to whether they flower long or only once, whether they are tall or short, or are climbers, ramblers, standards and what not. In this way I hope my readers will be able to find the information they require, and if the search be a little tiresome amid such a wealth of items, very possibly the search itself may prove not unpleasurable.

And while we are on the subject, I would advise all those about to plant—especially if it's their first attempt—to take a look round our public parks and nursery-gardens; to read, mark, learn and try to obtain reliable information as to which kinds or sorts are best suited for that special spot in your garden, or for the conditions prevailing in your part of the world, *before* making a final selection.

We must also consider the colour question, for it is not all roses that match each other equally well. There was a time *before* all the new bright reds, yellows and oranges coloured our roses—a time when they were either red, pink or white, or intermediary shades of these. The reds of those days often had a bluish tinge and this mattered not a jot, for all the colours were of the same family and therefore suited each other. The crimson and bluish tones merely served to make the reds still more lively.

It was the old Centifolia Damask and Bourbon roses that most possessed this quality. If you wish to have both of these categories in your garden each must be planted by itself. But there are also other and newer sorts, like General MacArthur or Red Riding Hood which it is unwise to plant among sorts like Karen, Cocorico, Ena Harkness, etc. Park roses look their best standing alone among low perennials or alpines—or in front, among flowering bushes. And the same holds good of many of the vigorous hybrid polyanthas. But naturally the question of the right colour combination is a matter of taste. Some people like to plant all the reds in a single group and let the various shades form their own symphony, planting another group with light, or with yellow and orange shades. The whites on the other hand, are not difficult to neutralise.

I have ventured to touch upon this point, as many rose-growers nowadays try more and more to produce roses with pure strong colours. At the same time I have deleted a former special section on bushy perpetuals, the contents being dealt with partly in various parts of the book describing individual sorts, and partly in this present section.

Ramblers and climbers

The fourth and not least important group among our modern garden roses. Earlier we described their descent, pruning and cultivation. In this section I shall therefore mention only their use and position in a garden.

1. RAMBLERS SUITABLE FOR TRAINING OVER A PERGOLA, FOR PLANTING AS A SOLITARY PILLAR OR NEAR A HEDGE. Sorts marked with a (*W*) are Wichuraiana hybrids which have glossy, longlasting foliage.

AGLAIA. Small, full, greenish-yellow. Is very vigorous and floriferous if pruned gently and allowed to keep its long lateral shoots, these being merely thinned out and trimmed.

ALBERTINE (*W*). Copper-yellow, quite large flowers, resembles a tea-rose, fragrant.

AMERICAN PILLAR. Deep-red with white centre; the blooms are single and set in large clusters. It is one of the very best and most hardy of the ramblers and is therefore a much planted sort.

BLAZE. Scarlet, semi-double, large-flowered. It is a constant-flowering sport of the well-known and much planted Paul's Scarlet Climber.

CARPET OF GOLD (*W*). Recent American sort. Vigorous with attractively glossy, green foliage. This rose is exceptionally free-flowering and is then densely covered with a profusion of small shapely golden-yellow blooms. It is very useful as an espaliered rose against a fence or for covering slopes. It has a delightful perfume.

CHAPLIN'S PINK CLIMBER. Light pink, semi-double and somewhat continuous. A healthy, prolific sort.

CLIMBING AMERICAN BEAUTY (*W*). Vigorous climber, up to three or four yards in height, with rather large, full, fragrant warm-pink blooms.

CLIMBING MME CAROLINE TESTOUT. A climber sport of the well-known hybrid tea of the same name. It blooms in autumn, at a time when all other climbers have faded and fallen.

CLIMBING CRIMSON GLORY. Another climbing hybrid tea which has proved to be vigorous, hardy and floriferous, with the large delightful deep-red, fragrant blooms so characteristic of this variety.

CLIMBING GOLDILOCKS. Is a climbing form of the yellow polyantha rose that is so much planted in America. It is healthy, very floriferous and blooms continuously and vigorously all summer through.

CLIMBING KAREN POULSEN. Also a vigorous climbing sport of the well-known brilliant red polyantha, Karen Poulsen.

Besides the climbing forms named above, partly of large-flowered garden roses and partly of polyanthas, a very large selection is given in most foreign catalogues, of which some may possibly be found to be hardy in this country [Denmark]. But they will have to be tried first before it would be advisable to recommend them for general planting in our Northern climate.

COUNTESS SYLVIA KNUTH (W). White with yellowish centre, in large clusters of Dorothy Perkins type.

DR W. VAN FLEET (Hybrid setigera). Light flesh-colour, full, large-flowered. Undoubtedly the most hardy and also the most vigorously sprouting climber we have in this country. It is also immune from mildew.

DOROTHY PERKINS (W). Salmon-pink, very full, in large clusters up to twelve feet high, sweetly scented. It was with the appearance of this lovely rose that the then new Wichuraiana hybrids became famous.

DOUBLOONS. A Setigera hybrid of American raising. A very robust and vigorous climber, carrying large, dark-yellow blooms in clusters.

EASLEA'S GOLDEN RAMBLER (W). Pure, yellow large-flowered, a very beautiful and prolific sort.

EXCELSA (W). Clear red, small-flowered, but with large clusters of the same type as Dorothy Perkins.

FRAGEZEICHEN. Pink, large-flowered, moderate grower.

GRÜSS AUS ZABERN. Pure white, strong grower, floriferous and very fragrant.

MAGIC CARPET (W). A new-comer, with large full blooms. A beautiful tea-rose type, yellow with shades of orange, scarlet and pink. A very charming, brilliant-coloured climber, and very durable.

NEW DAWN. Light flesh-coloured large-flowered, a continuous-flowering sport of Dr van Fleet.

PAUL'S SCARLET CLIMBER. Scarlet, large-flowered, semi-double and prolific. Is a sort that is much planted at present and is often seen on fences and pergolas in suburban gardens.

PRIMEVÈRE. Has small, dark yellow, tea-rose shaped, elegant, fragrant blooms and an exceptionally fine display.

SANDER'S WHITE (W). Pure white, full, Dorothy Perkins type.

TAUSENDSCHÖN. Chaste pink, large-flowered with curling petals; the growth is moderate, leaves and branches are light, glossy and almost thornless.

THELMA. Pink, with cream-yellow shadings. Blooms in clusters. An exceptionally strong and floriferous rambler.

TURNER'S CRIMSON RAMBLER. Carmine, large clusters of blooms and exceptionally floriferous. Was originally brought from Japan, and at once roused quite a furore among rose-growers. Is, however, not so much planted now, as it has proved rather susceptible to mildew.

2. CLIMBERS, SUITABLE FOR WALLS

Some of these have already been mentioned in earlier sections, partly as being suitable for other purposes, and partly as being among those which should only be planted against a wall, as they need a warm and sheltered situation. Walls facing south or west are always better than against a wall facing east which, as a rule, gets too dry; but it is always advisable to water any roses planted against a wall especially well. The † opposite the names of some of the following varieties refers the reader to the pruning method mentioned in the section dealing with espalier roses.

ALBERTINE (*W*). Copper-yellow, described above.

†BOUQUET D'OR (Noisette). Dark-yellow on a copper-coloured ground. Large-flowered and a very strong grower.

†CHARLES BONNET (perpetual). Tender pink, fragrant, and a wealth of bloom in spring and autumn.

CLIMBING AMERICAN BEAUTY. Zinnober-pink, full, vigorous and hardy.

†CLIMBING MME CAROLINE TESTOUT. Hybrid tea, mentioned earlier.

CLIMBING CRIMSON GLORY. Deep-red, large-flowered, mentioned earlier.

CLIMBING GOLDILOCKS. Yellow, small-flowered polyantha. Mentioned earlier.

CLIMBING PEACE. A very vigorous and robust espalier rose with the same glorious blooms as those on the Peace described among the hybrid teas. It is, however, not specially floriferous.

DR W. VAN FLEET. Light flesh-coloured, vigorous. Mentioned earlier.

Above left : Luna   *Above right : Roselandia*

Below : Heidekind

Above left : Mrs Pierre S. Dupont
Below left : Ophelia

Above right : Poulsen's Pink
Below right : Crimson Glory

†DOUBLOONS. Dark yellow, large-flowered. Mentioned earlier.

EASLEA'S GOLDEN RAMBLER. Yellow. Mentioned earlier.

FORTUNE'S DOUBLE YELLOW. The first yellow tea-rose to be introduced from China. It is completely hardy, slender of growth, flowers early fragrant and continuous-flowering.

†GLOIRE DE DIJON (tea-rose). Salmon-yellow with shades of pink, sweet-smelling with long vigorous shoots. A well-known old-fashioned sort.

†PHYLLIS BIDE. Light yellow and pink, constant-flowering. Mentioned earlier.

†PRIMEVÈRE. Dark yellow. Mentioned earlier.

†REINE MARIE HENRIETTE (tea-rose). Pretty cherry-red, long shapely buds, long vigorous stems.

†RÊVE D'OR (Noisette). Leather-yellow, fragrant, large-flowered, long vigorous shoots.

†ROYAL SCARLET HYBRID. Dark scarlet, shapely, large-flowered. Mentioned earlier.

†SOUVENIR DE CLAUDIUS DENOYEL (hybrid tea). An exceptionally beautiful, large-flowered, shapely rose, with erect shoots, and a constant-flowering, deep-red display.

†WILLIAM ALLEN RICHARDSON (Noisette). Bright saffron, medium height, very charming rose. Very floriferous, with erect shoots. An espalier rose that can be recommended to any grower who will spend the time and labour on tending it. It must stand in the most sheltered spot in the garden, and must be protected, in winter, with pine twigs. It is an old-fashioned sort that was formerly extremely popular.

I

CHAPTER EIGHT

Old-Fashioned Garden Roses

THESE ROSES WERE MUCH FAVOURED SOME TWENTY-FIVE YEARS AGO. They are still planted today and have their own patrons and admirers. But they have been largely ousted by more popular, healthier (though not always more beautiful), more fragrant and hardier sorts. Yet they deserve to be planted still—if not in great numbers—in borders and groupings in the rose-garden or in the mixed-border reserved for vase decoration.

Hybrid perpetuals

The majority of these roses are taller, more thorny and their leaves are less smooth than the modern garden-roses described above. They are also more susceptible to rose-rust, and especially the dark-red varieties, if they are not thoroughly sprayed with Bordeaux mixture several times during summer, will give only a single real display, namely the first, and the rest of the summer will stand leafless and without flowers. The light-red and medium-red kinds are less suceptible, more prolific and, even on a poor, sandy soil, will do better than most other large-flowered varieties. In addition to the various sorts already mentioned under Modern Garden Roses the following may be recommended.

ALFRED COLOMB. Large, fiery-red, floriferous and fragrant.

BARONNE DE ROTHSCHILD. Pink, extra large flowers, erect growth.

CAPTAIN CHRISTY. Flesh-coloured, large-flowered, close, erect growth.

DR ANDRY. Brilliant dark-crimson, shapely and sweetly scented.

FISHER HOLMES. Dark scarlet, fragrant, and have a wealth of bloom in autumn.

FRAU KARL DRUSCHKI (Snow Queen). See under Large-flowered Garden Roses.

GENERAL JACQUEMINOT. Lively, velvety scarlet, fragrant, vigorous growth.

GEORGE DICKSON. Deep dark-red, very large flowers and fragrant. A much favoured exhibition rose among British amateur exhibitors, mainly on account of the large flowers and their shapely form.

HUGH DICKSON. See under Large-flowered Garden Roses.

MADAME GABRIEL LUIZET. See under Large-flowered Garden Roses.

MRS JOHN LAING. See under Large-flowered Garden Roses.

MRS G. R. SHARMAN CRAWFORD. A wonderfully floriferous, chaste-pink, strong-scented rose of peerless form.

PAUL NEYRON. Dark pink, strongly perfumed, vigorously erect, healthy growth and enormous flowers.

The Monthly Roses (the Bengal roses)

Have now been completely ousted by our more robust and hardier polyanthas. Formerly the selection grown was relatively large; now there is only one single variety left, and this is probably being still retained only for sentimental reasons, but also, I think, because there really was something good about the old Monthly roses. Like the polyanthas of today, they were much planted in the old days, and their popularity continued until about 1900 when they were supplanted by the former.

In recent years a whole series of quite small but delightful miniature roses have appeared, that have been raised from *Rosa Rouletii* by cross-breeding it with the large-flowered hybrid teas. Attempts at fixing the miniature form were successful, and they really are most enchanting, these tiny roselets, which can now be obtained in great variety, in many different shades and of as perfect shape as the best of the hybrid teas. They somehow do not seem to suit either in an ordinary rose-bed or indeed in the rose-garden at all. They should rather be planted by themselves in miniature beds, in the crazy pavement, on the terrace or in the rockery, in well-tilled, not too heavy soil. They are also well suited for indoor decoration in flower-pots.

BABY GOLD. Miniature yellow tea-rose.

GABRIELLE PRIVET. Slightly taller, small flowered, pink.

PERLE D'ALCANADA. Cochineal-red, small, semi-double, very floriferous, dark, glossy foliage.

ROULETII (*Rosa rouletii* or Miss Lawrance's rose, also Pompon de Paris). Is the smallest roselet of all, being only four to six inches in height. It has a profusion of small pink blooms.

Large-flowered roses of yesterday and the day before

It may still be quite useful to know these old-fashioned roses. Properly planted they may be 'a thing of beauty and a joy forever' and they are certainly of excellent effect in almost any garden. They are completely hardy. They may be used to frame the rose-garden by putting them in among other bushy perpetuals. They may be used as front-figure plants, too, in front of flowering shrubs, and here, weighed down by their wealth of bloom, will sway out towards the lawn or garden-path. Or, with certain sorts, they may be trained up as espalier plants along low fences or wire railings. Indeed, almost all the same uses as those to which more modern ramblers may be put.

They require plenty of room, however, if they are to fully develop their individual characteristics. Otherwise, in their struggle for light and air, they will crowd each other out, and thus form leggy, straggling bushes. They are thus of little use in a small garden. As to pruning, see above.

CENTIFOLIA (*Rosa centifolia major*). The true Provence rose, brilliant pink, large, full, very fragrant.

CENTIFOLIA ALBA. A towering, light-leaved and light-barked plant that is therefore supposed to be a species of Damask rose. It is white, large-flowered and fragrant.

CELLINI (*Rosa alba*). Splendid, large-flowered blooms set in large clusters, good for espalier and for bushy beds. The large, open, double, blushing-pink blooms exhale a strong but delightful fragrance.

CELESTIAL (*Rosa alba*). Same type as Cellini; it forms a tall bush with large, greyish leaves and pretty pink blooms. Well suited for espalier and bushy beds.

COUPE D'HÉBÉ (Bourbon rose). With its characteristic, round, bun-like buds and its charming, shell-shaped, open blooms, it is, possibly, the most beautiful of all the old roses. The growth is vigorous and healthy, and it may form very large bushes. It is highly floriferous, carrying three or four blooms on each stalk. The colour is a warm pink and the perfume is rich and full-bodied.

GREAT WESTERN (Bourbon rose). Chaste pink, floriferous, hardy.

LOUIS ODIER (Bourbon rose). Lovely shade of pink, medium size, fragrant, vigorous growth.

MADAME PLANTIER (Damask). Light green foliage and light bark; forms a tall, dense, thickly branched bush. I have seen it planted as a hedge over a stone wall where it formed a broad overhanging flower-bedecked barrier weighed down by its profusion of medium-sized pure-white blooms.

MAIDEN'S BLUSH (*Rosa alba*). Light flesh-coloured pink, medium-sized, flat, densely filled blooms. This is another of the good old profusely blooming roses which will live on through the ages.

PAUL RICAULT (Damask rose). Large, well filled, brilliant carmine pink and very floriferous.

QUEEN OF DENMARK. Flesh-coloured pink with a blushing centre and with a wealth of shapely densely-filled blooms.

SOUVENIR DE VICTOR LANDEAU (Bourbon rose). Lively-red shaded with carmine, large, firm, sweet-scented blooms, free-flowering and vigorous.

SOUVENIR DE LA MALMAISON (Bourbon rose). Chaste creamy white, very floriferous and flowers over long period, healthy and vigorous.

The moss-roses

And in conclusion, a word or two on these roses formerly so popular, which still have their admirers. Moss-roses should be grown in much the same way as other garden roses, if they are to be fully enjoyed. They must be thinned out and pruned, be manured, watered and sprayed if you want them to put forth their really large, beautiful, mossy blooms.

COMMON RED MOSS-ROSE. Possibly the most attractive of all; dark blushing pink, very mossy and fragrant.

BLANCHE MOREAU. Pure white, floriferous, with extra mossy buds.

CIRISTATA. Pink, fragrant, extra mossy sepals.

HENRY MARTIN. Brilliant red, fragrant.

SALET. Pink, thickly covered with moss.

This concludes the lists of roses which according to my taste and experience are most worthy of mention. Very possibly other rose specialists would have liked me to include other and quite different sorts and varieties. Yet though I meant to cut down the number far more than I have done

I fear I have not succeeded as well as I should have liked. Nor do I wish to recommend my readers to plant their gardens from A to Z with those I have included.

But it is to be hoped that my remarks may be of some use and guidance to an odd reader or two, even if all they need is just a single plant, or merely a couple or so.

CHAPTER NINE

Rose Gardens and their General Layout

Mixed plantings with perennials and roses

PLANTING ROSES IN PERENNIAL BORDERS, or planting such perennials as form a good background in the rose-border, is a good way of getting a better colour effect and a greater and more striking variety of bloom than might otherwise have been possible for either, when planted alone. The most suitable roses for this kind of combination-planting are the free-flowering hybrid polyanthas.

In a perennial border, which should preferably be of a certain size, say six feet broad by thirty feet long, the problem is not difficult to solve. Plant your roses in groups of three or even more, beginning, for instance, with some pink varieties at one end of the bed and passing gradually over to yellow and orange in the middle, and finishing off at the far end with some strong red varieties. In between, in front, and behind the roses, put in your perennials according to colour, so that they harmonise with the roses near them, and at the same time varying their time of flowering so that the bed will be in bloom before, during, and after the roses have finished their display.

As to the sorts of roses that would be suitable for this kind of arrangement, I would suggest beginning with some pink Crown Princess Ingrid,

Else Poulsen, Poulsen's Fairy as well as Betty Prior, which are all tall and prolific. For dwarf kinds for the foreground there are Ellen Poulsen, Grethe Poulsen, Nathalie Nypels, Heidekind and several others. Among the perennials that would match these, you might put in some of the following tall varieties: light blue and pink lupins, light blue larkspurs, *Salvia nemorosa* (sage), *Aconitum* (Monkshood), *Echinops* (Globe Thistle), *Anchusa* (Alkanet), *Erigeron* (Flea Bane), and, possibly, for late autumn flowering, some *Solidago* (Golden Rod) and white and blue starworts.

In front of and between the roses you might put in some dwarf *Aster amellus*, lavender, *Nepeta* (Catmint), *Stachys lanata* (Lamb's Tongue), *Aster alpinus* (6 in. Starwort), as well as some cushiony alpine pinks and Aubretia (Purple Rock Cress) in the very front. And if you also put in plenty of the two white lilies, *Candidum* and *Regale*, and some *gypsophila paniculata* (Chalk plant) you will greatly enhance the general effect.

Continuing with the pink-coloured roses you might plant some white or faintly pink varieties like Irene, Grüss an Aachen and Danish Gold. It is not difficult to find transition colours among the perennials to match these white roses, for, among the lupins and irises there are plenty of suitable intermediary colours. Blue larkspurs, too, and white and pink Japanese autumn anemones (windflowers) and a few autumn starworts would not come amiss; and then possibly you might have

some green *Festuca crinumurse* (Fescue Grass) to
further enhance the effect. You must remember
that your main object is to emphasise the colour
of your roses by rightly choosing the flowers
around them. That is why phloxes are wholly
banned from our selection. The roses will be
there instead and have the advantage that they
flower for a longer period than do any phloxes.

Among the yellow and orange-yellow hybrid
polyanthas there are not many that are suitable
over and above Golden Orange, Poulsen's Copper
and maybe Fashion. Among the perennials,
however, there are first and foremost, the pure
yellow, long-flowering *Coreopsis verticillata* (Tick-
seed), and in the foreground some *Oenothera
missouriensis* (Evening Primrose), and some yellow
and brown irises and lupins of like colour; and
then for intermediary colours; some reddish lupins
and poppies. Finally, we might put in the reds,
beginning with the lighter tones of Kirsten Poulsen,
Karen Poulsen, the darker red Ellen Poulsen,
Donald Prior and Joseph Guy.

To match these, some red-flowering *Heuchera*
(Alum root), *Rudbeckia purpurea* (cone flower) and
Monarda (Horse mint) would be just the thing.
But kinds like *Lychnis* (Campion) should be carefully avoided; their sealingwax-red lacks the
smallest tinge of blue and thus makes a dishar-
monious contrast to the warm crimsons of the
roses, which all have a slightly bluish touch. On
the other hand, yellow perennials like *Rudbeckia*

speciosa, Coreopsis verticillata and *Solidago* (Golden Rod) make a lovely contrast.

The above suggestions for arranging a mixed rose-cum-perennial border are, of course, merely intended as a rough outline, which may be varied *ad lib* according to taste and inclination.

Box and other edging plants that may be used in the rose-garden with good effect

Most roses—especially the taller sorts, and among these again the perpetuals most of all— have an unfortunate tendency to lose their lower foliage as summer advances, and whether you may like to call this drawback 'bare-stemmed, legginess' or pure cussedness, it is undoubtedly not a be- coming feature. That roses often discard a good proportion of their leaves in dry periods is only natural. Like other plants they are merely trying to arrive at a balance between water supply and consumption.

Gardeners have always tried to mitigate this unbecoming feature of the rose-garden by planting low 'hedges' or edging plants round their rose- beds. I well remember the time when this edging often consisted of trimmed oak hedgings. This style has now—fortunately—been abandoned. The oaklets got out of hand and developed mildew. On the other hand, low box edging has not yet gone entirely out of fashion. Possibly this is due to the fact that box, in itself, is such a trim little plant and indeed one of the very best we have for edging.

But everything may be overdone. There was a time when one got the impression that the box edging was the most important part of a rose-bed. Hence the vigorous reaction—which almost did away with poor little box for good.

But where sensibly and tastefully employed, and when beds and pathways are the right size and shape, box is still right and reasonable. If everything is as it should be the visiting public can walk right up to every individual rose, bend down over it, and enjoy to the full the appearance and perfume of each variety.

There are all sorts of sizes and shapes of rose-gardens, and each must be designed and laid out by an architect-gardener, but one feature is common to them all: it must be possible to get at the beds from all sides and reach the plants in the middle without having to trample on the bed to do so.

Roses must be trimmed and tended, but the soil must never be trodden firm between them, if they are not to lose their vigour and vitality. If you will look at professionals' illustrations of some rose-beds in a lawn you will note that the lawn is surrounded by wild, and other kinds of bush roses, while the beds themselves are planted with *Nepeta Musinii* (Catmint) among the roses. The framing round each bed consists of a double row of old railway sleepers, the one outside being dug down on edge, the inside one lying flat.

In addition to box there are plenty of low perennials that are suitable partly as edging plants and partly as screening plants round leggy roses. These should be selected so that the colour of the leaves and flowers harmonises well with that of the roses. Among these I would specially recommend the low, grey-leaved, cushiony pinks, *Acaena Buchananii* (New Zealand bur), *Stachys lanata* (Lamb's Tongue), grey and green Fescue grass and others of similar growth and character.

Even quite tall perennials and flowering bushes are sometimes planted in among garden roses, or behind as a background, without the garden losing in character. On the contrary, they will often help to emphasise the contrasting colour effects between the roses and themselves. Ellen Poulsen, for instance, when viewed against a background of Larkspurs and *Salvia nemorosa* (Sage). Or, as in our next-door neighbour's garden, where Kirsten Poulsen is planted in two long rows behind hedges of lavender flanking the drive up to the house. In both cases a really charming colour effect has been provided.

Incidentally, it is the same perennials as those mentioned in my description of the mixed rose-cum-perennial border, that may be used in the rose-garden, supplemented maybe, with some flowering bushes like Buddleia, garden fuchsias, *Hypericum patulum* (St. John's Wort) and *Sambucus canadensis maxima* (Canadian elderberry).

The 'right' choice of kinds and colours depends ultimately, of course, on the personal taste either of the landscape architect or of the amateur who prefers to arrange and plant his garden himself. But that roses are used and planted far more freely today than ever they were before, and are not confined strictly to a rose-bed or rose-garden any more is because they are so good today and vary so delightfully in form, colour, growth and type that it is evident that they are better in every way than they have ever been before.

In a rose-collector's garden

In the cottage garden plan reproduced facing page 145 (scale 1:200) it is suggested that the garden be planted almost entirely with roses. Only bed No. 24 (on the same sketch (scale 1:200)) is to be planted with perennials, consisting mainly of larkspurs, irises, lilies, sage (*nemorosa*) and dwarf autumn asters (*amellus*) and stonecrop (*sedum spectabile*).

In the borders along the fence bulb plants may be put in, but if so, must be planted so deep that they will not hamper work in the garden during summer.

The garden is surrounded by a wooden fence stretching from the gate northward along the eastern and southern sides. As far as the covered-in outdoor lounge in the south-western corner, it may be about four feet high (though it may well be as much as six feet if so desired) while the posts for the pergola (which should be of larch) should be about eight feet. The beds are edged with clinkers. There are flagstones or crazy pavement round the house and underfoot in the outdoor lounge. The path through the pergola is gravel while the rest of the area is sown with grass.

Scheme of planting (as per numbering on plan facing page 145)

1: twelve Mrs Pierre S. du Pont. 2: twelve Michèle Meilland. 3: twelve Ena Harkness. 4: eight Luis de Brinas. 5: seven McGredy's Sunset. 6: nine Peace. 7: nine Grande Duchesse Charlotte. 8: seven Mme Butterfly. 9: twelve Tallyho. 10: four Spek's Yellow. 11*a* is planted, for eleven yards in all, with the vigorous, dark-red polyantha Frensham (which should be trimmed only lightly) in two rows with fourteen plants in each row. 11, 11*b* and *d*: the back row is planted with the *rugosa* roses: Frau Dagmar Hastrup and *Stella Polaris* with twelve of each planted indiscriminately with three feet between each plant. The front row is planted with the following vigorous hybrid polyanthas, with one and a half feet between varieties: Fanal, Orange Triumph, Kirsten Poulsen, Baroness Manon, Mrs Julie Poulsen, Poulsen's Fairy, Poulsen's Supreme, Poulsen's Bedder, Betty Prior, Cocorico, Poulsen's Pink and Poulsen's Crimson two of each sort. For the first few years before the roses develop, there will be room for a few tufts of lavender and sage (*Salvia nemorosa*). 12: three *Rosa Moyesii*. 12*a*: three *Rosa Nevada*.

Sun

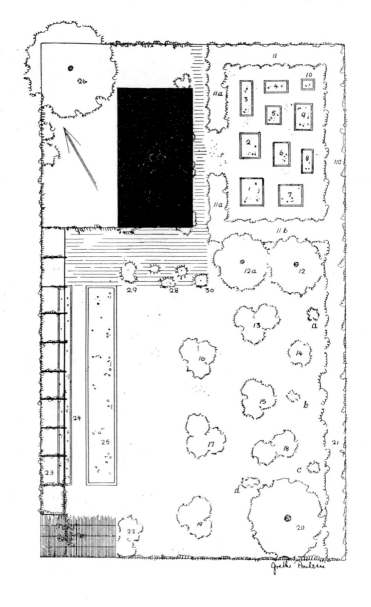

Grete Poulsen

13: three *Rosa Hugonis*. 14: one *Rosa setipoda*. 15: three *Rosa cantabrigiensis*. 16: one D. T. Poulsen's Park Rose. 17: three *Rosa humilis*. 18: two *Rosa sericia pteracantha*. 19: three *Rosa highdownensis*. 20: one standard purple 'Clammy Locust' (*Robinia viscosa*). *a*: one *Rosa Andersonii*. *b*: one *Rosa canina Mosvig*. *c*: one *Rosa Wardii culta*. *d*: one Rosa Frühlingsgold. 21: is planted with old-fashioned garden-roses, fifteen in all, one of each; beginning from the northern end: Mme Plantier, *Rosa alba*, common Red Moss-rose, Queen of Denmark, Celestial, Centifolia, Coupe d'Hébé, Paul Ricault, Maiden's Blush, Moss-rose Henry Martin, Cellini, *Rosa multiflora*, *Rosa rubiginosa refulgens*, *Rosa spinosissima altaica*, *Rosa carolina*.

The low fence facing south is planted with rambling perpetuals (with about six feet between plants), which must be tied up along the fence. The following are suggested: Hamburg, New Dawn, Phyllis Bide, and Blaze.

22: two *Rosa Wardii culta*. 23: the western side of the pergola abuts on the six-foot high wooden fence, which may be planted with honeysuckle and large-flowered clematis, the posts of the pergola (beginning at the southern end) being planted with ramblers in the following order (one for each post: Dr W. van Fleet, which is of a sufficiently climbing nature to also cover the covered-in lounge as well, then: Chaplin's Pink Climber, Aglaia, American Pillar, Primevère,

K

Fragezeichen, Sanders' White, Thelma, Paul's Scarlet Climber, Tausendschön, and Grüss aus Zabern.

The fence round the courtyard is planted with some completely hardy Sweet Briar or Eglantine (*Rosa rubiginosa*) which, when trained along it as espalier-roses will look like ramblers; in between these, three or four different varieties of large-flowered clematis may well be planted. 26: in the corner is another wattle (*Robinia Pseudacaesa semperflorens*).

Near the house, on the south side, some less hardy espalier roses may be put in, e.g.: William Allen Richardson and Souvenir de Claudius Denovel. On the west side: Rêve d'Or, Doubloons and Belle Vichysoise, and on the north side: Charles Bonnet.

28: among the flags round the house, some dwarf *Rosa rouletii* may be planted, with tufts of Aubretia in between. 30: three Grete Poulsen with *Campanula portenschlagiana* in between.

25: the rose-bed will be described in detail on page 147.

Naturally this garden may well be planted quite differently and with other sorts. Or maybe either with fewer, or with many more of the varieties named. In this design we have tried, in spite of the great number of items the garden contains, to provide for a quiet, collective whole.

1.   7 Ellen Poulsen.
2.   8 Irene.
3.   4 Alain.
4.   7 Poulsen's Yellow.
5.   4 Karl Weinhausen.
6.   11 Poinsettia.
7.   4 Poulsen's Copper.
8.   11 Grüss an Aachen.
9.   4 Margo Koster.
10.   7 Else Poulsen, mildew-proof.
11.   11 Crown Princess Ingrid.
12.   5 Innocence.
13.   10 Hector Deane.
14.   6 Roselandia.
15.   10 Ophelia.
16.   7 Elite.
17.   10 Mevrouw G. A. van Rossem.
18.   7 Eclipse.
19.   4 Gretel Greul.
20.   4 Briarcliff.
21.   11 Dainty Bess.
22.   4 Inge Poulsen.
23.   8 Karen Poulsen.
24.   4 Betty Uprichard.
25.   9 Heidekind.
26.   7 Mevrouw Nathalie Nypels.
27.   7 Fashion.

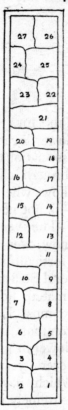

CHAPTER TEN

Rose Societies and Cultivation of Exhibition Roses

THE IDEA OF HORTICULTURISTS, gardeners and flower lovers getting together in clubs and various associations so as to exchange ideas—perhaps through club periodicals, or by holding flower shows where 'the perfect specimen' can be judged —is not new in this country.

The venerable Danish Horticultural Society (now over a hundred years old), the Østifterne's Horticultural Society, and the Juttish Horticultural Society—the majority of whose members are amateur flower or garden enthusiasts—are known to most Danes, but for people to unite out of common interest in the cultivation of a single flower or plant variety is of later date—though, for several years, we have had a chrysanthemum club, which has organised quite comprehensive and extremely interesting shows.

There was also, for a time, an Orchid society, and now, quite recently the newly founded Dahlia society which seems to thrive and enrol many new and enthusiastic members. Otherwise I know of no other Danish societies of that kind in this country, with the exception of the Danish Lathyrus and Rose Society—which was founded in 1939. The member list of this Society proves that by far the greater number of its members are amateurs. This is perhaps because the main aims and objects of this Society are firstly the skilful training of members, and secondly the giving of prizes for the best flowers grown by amateurs. The judging of entries takes place at the annual exhibitions, which have generally been held in the Royal Horticultural Society's Gardens. But, to my sorrow, I have just learnt that this Society has been obliged to close its doors. Whether this untimely demise is to be laid at the door of the management, or is due to a saddening lack of interest on the part of garden-owners, is not easy to decide. However that may be, one thing is certain: in spite of this unfortunate set-back, the general interest in Roses has in no way slackened off. On the contrary, I would suggest that in Denmark, and indeed in Nordic countries as a whole, far more roses are being planted per head of population than in most other countries, England included.

In reality, all over the world, the idea is quite an old one. For centuries the Japanese have had Chrysanthemum clubs, and have, indeed, the oldest society in the world for extolling the praises of their ethereal cherry-blossom.

Among Rose societies, the British National Rose Society is the oldest (founded 1870) having a present membership of over 40,000 spread all over the world, everywhere where Englishmen have settled. The Society has its own experimental trial ground at St. Albans, and rose-growers the world over may send their novelties there to be tested under similar conditions over a two- or three-year period, which is usually followed by a final judging at the annual exhibition in London in June or July.

Similar societies having the same interests and similar working methods, and having their own rosariums, are to be found in many countries. Verein Deutscher Rosenfreunde (founded 1883) has its own extensive and very valuable rosarium at Sangerhausen, which contains an amazing assortment both of old-time roses as well as new-comers, all precisely arranged according to species and origin, and including also, possibly the largest collection of wild roses from all parts of the world. The gardens of this Society are now in the East Zone, and it is doubtful how they are weathering the storm. But the Germans have a further two excellent rosariums, one near a small town called Uetersen in Holstein, not far from Hamburg; and the other in the Planten und Blomen Gardens in Hamburg itself.

Then there is the American Rose Society which, in addition to the above aims and objects, also works to establish Municipal Rose Gardens in every town of importance in the States.

There are, moreover, French, Spanish, Italian and Australian Rose societies, and there was at one time a Danish Rose Society as well.

It can hardly be denied that all these Rose societies signify a growing interest in, and a spreading knowledge of rose-growing in general, but my own view is that their most important function is to enable members to participate in exhibitions, and to promote that intimate relationship between rose and grower that can only be acquired by studying the details of their growth and make up. The cultivation of roses gives the practitioner one of the greatest and purest joys this world has to offer. If one is ever to get the length of exhibiting roses one must be able to cultivate them in the right way—as should be plain from the contents of this book. To this must be added a knowledge of certain special tricks, such as, for instance, that of cutting a rose hard back when spring pruning, in order to obtain larger and more vigorous flowers, or in the case of polyanthas, larger flower-clusters. Or that of timing one's pruning correctly; or choosing the right bud, or several buds, that are to bloom on the day of the Show. The weather, too, may vary from year to year; one year May is warm and dry, another year it is June, or perhaps both months are dry and hot, as opposed to last year when they were cold and rainy. No definite rule can be given. But four or five weeks before the day of the Show thinning must be begun, and continued in such a way that a richly varying selection of rose-buds in different stages of maturity have been secured. When the middle bud is the size of a pea all the side buds must be pinched off, taking every care not to damage the all-important middle bud.

Should it be thought likely that the roses will bloom too early, this middle bud may be removed and one of the smaller lateral buds kept instead. This will then develop normally and vigorously as it will receive all the rising sap and thus be brought to bloom a whole week later.

In this case it is advisable, however, after having removed the middle bud, to let the two nearest buds remain *in situ* for a few days, so as to be sure that the bud selected is normally developed.

A downright deformity of development may result from suddenly removing all the buds but that one tender little lateral bud: being suddenly forced to absorb all the rising sap, it may well be twisted quite awry.

Truly it may be said, in clutivating roses, as in so many other occupations, experience is the father of wisdom, memory the mother.

Attention to watering, fertilisers, liquid manure, mulching, and digging the soil at least one spit deep, are not the least of the many important duties that must never be scamped. Care must be taken, too, that insect and other pests are not allowed to gain a footing, or that mildew does not mar the foliage. All of which are just as important to the health and well-being of your roses as it is in the eyes of the judges when assessing the value of the finished product.

The day of the Show draws ever nearer. And as it does so the more anxious do you become as to whether the right moment for disbudding or thinning has arrived. It would indeed be strange if some of your best blooms did not flower too early. If it is a question of only one or two days, they may possibly still be saved. Late at night, or early in the morning while the dew is still on the leaves, if your rose-buds have begun to feel slightly soft, but before they begin to burst, they should be detached with good long stalks, the buds tied in with a soft woollen thread, and the cut flowers immersed deep in water, and stored in a cool, dark cellar. With luck they may keep long enough to be used together with other later blooms that may be cut the same morning early before the Show opens.

These disbudding operations cannot, of course, be used with polyanthas or ramblers whose greatest beauty depends on the size and fullness of their flower-clusters and on the health and gloss of their surrounding foliage.

How such a Rose Show should be arranged, will naturally depend upon the programme set for the various groups. In one, many specially well-developed specimens of a single sort may be required. In another, a collection of various sorts with only few specimens in each vase, may be the order of the day. Or, again, exhibitors may wish to compete for the most beautifully arranged basket or vase in the Show, or for the most beautiful table decoration.

However that may be, it is always enjoyable and indeed profitable, to take part in them, for with every attendance one has bettered one's acquaintance with, and further extended one's knowledge of this the World's most beautiful blossom. There is an old Swedish ditty that says:

> *Muck is muck, and snuff is snuff,*
> *E'en it in gold reposes;*
> *And roses in some cheap cracked stuff*
> *Are still and always roses!*

Index